Praise f<

Pimping My

When I first heard Amador bless the mic with "My Little Bitch," he captured the essence of darkness, giving it form, emotions, and voice. For the first time, I met someone who understood the complex ethereality of trauma and the seductive assimilation of darkness. Pimping My Trauma takes the reader through a journey of his origin; battling the sinister entanglement with deep and darkened humorous lines, accepts the hostile truth, and finally, rediscovers self-ascension and hope. Juan Amador is comfortably unapologetic and confronts toxic masculinity head on, taking no prisoners, though releasing them.

–VOTH | Voice of the Harbor, Author of Dieagnosis

"To say that Juan Amador tackles the subject of male vulnerability would not tell the full story. Juan tackles the subject of male vulnerability from the top of a steel cage, and slams it through a pile of thumbtacks. But not all at once. The poems in Pimping My Trauma do not speak of quick and easy victories. They speak of drawn-out struggle and startling strength, of getting back to your feet despite low blows and outside interference. They speak of breaking the headlock grip of toxic masculinity, generational trauma, the social pressures that contribute to struggles with healthy intimacy–and other topics that tend to shed their meaning when written about in abstract terms.

Juan does not write about these topics in abstract terms. Juan's poetry puts the "unvarnished" in "unvarnished truth." His natural humor surfaces and resurfaces no matter how many times it gets pulled under. Juan's poetry is down to earth, and off the wall. It is rising from the stretcher, crawling back into the ring–a steel folding chair gripped tight in its bruised, determined hands.

- Marc J. Cid

Juan Amador does not hold back in his poetry collection Pimping My Trauma. This collection exposes the haunting wounds of destructive masculinity, generational trauma, and even the chisme at family parties. Poems like "Emily", "Ghost Dancer", and "My Room" invite readers to connect with the dignity within and with each other no matter the self-inflicted scars nor the rain clouds that hover over our heads. Amador writes of his nightmares, his humanity, his salvation, and his courage to dream."

- Alex Petunia, Author of Tending My Wild

Pimping My Trauma

Pimping My Trauma

A Juan-of-a-Kind Collection of Poems and Proses

By Juan Amador

RIOT OF ROSES
PUBLISHING HOUSE
SEJATNGA
UNCEDED TONGVA TERRITORY
SOUTH WHITTIER, CALIFORNIA

Published by Riot of Roses Publishing House
Pimping My Trauma: A Juan-of-a-kind Collection of Poems and Proses

Copyright© 2024, Juan Amador
ISBN (paperback): 978-1-961717-22-0
ISBN (ebook): 978-1-961717-26-8
Library of Congress Control Number: 2024945544

Cover Artist© Elizabeth Weinschreider, 2024

First Edition, 2024

To request permissions, you may contact the Publisher
at riotofrosesllc@gmail.com

Printed in the United States of America.
www.riotofrosespublishinghouse.com
Cover design by Elizabeth Weinschreider
Cover Model: Juan Amador
Layout design by Waseem Aziz at www.arrowupz.com
Edited by Anne Marie Wells and Brenda Vaca
Editor-in-Chief Brenda Vaca

To the Little Boy in me
And all the survivors

Contents

Foreword

I first met Juan Amador three years ago at a poetry reading for Herencia de Café to celebrate Latino Heritage Month at El Cielito Café in South Gate. We were two of three poets sharing our work for this day to celebrate cultures with other artists and brown entrepreneurs. It was three years ago and the world was still navigating the precarious nature of living with el pinche covid and staying healthy. Many of us - though vaxxed - were still masking up, especially in more crowded spaces.

Only one of us had a published poetry collection. Mine was a couple of months away from publication - I was proudly carrying around the white covered proof. And the third poet, Juan Amador, was also joining the ranks of emerging poets during the early days of our poetic renaissance.

We each had a few minutes to share and I remember feeling awkward taking up space for poetry in the public square. I was the first one up and Juan followed. I remember being taken by his stage presence even in the middle of a bustling cafe in the heart of SELA (southeast Los Angeles) on Long Beach Blvd. It was especially moving because of the vulnerable nature of what Juan shared on the mic.

Over the last three years I've had the opportunity to share many mics with Juan Amador. Like many in the poetry scene of Southern California, I've seen Amador bloom and shine. One such occasion was when Juan showed up to a slam competition for a chance to be a performer on the main stage for Gothic Poetry Night 2 curated and hosted by former Bellator cage fighter, Jonathan Santa Maria.

A king of personification, Amador showed up with the white face of a mime, a top hat, and a long sleeve red shirt with black suspenders. He shared his widely recognized and celebrated poem, "My Little Bitch" to much enthusiasm from fellow poets and civilians (non-poets) alike. I remember being blown away at how much a person can shapeshift and transform in a short amount of time. Prior to this performance, Juan said after a mic, "We gotta keep evolving." It stayed with me because my favorite artists are those who are not afraid to tread into unknown waters for the sake of their craft.

Juan is not afraid to confront the truth of his trauma and his strength. At many times humorous and at other times achingly tender, the poet Amador knows how to capture his audience. And capture you he will in the pages of this book. The Poet weaves together surprising lines and biting self-reflection. One interesting thread that struck me as I made my way through this collection is the personification of inner strength in the face of adversity and demons - inner and outer - who dare rear their head on his journey toward integration and healing. The Poet becomes a mythological character who not only protects and saves his inner child, but also wields a literary sword before empire thinking and toxic masculinity.

Poems like "Machine Head," "Stoopid," and "Accent" are among my favorites with such lines as:

From "Machine Head":
"Somehow through his Sturm und Drang
We became prideful of our upbringing
Made us strong
We took hits
But kept going
We didn't complain
That's for pussies
People who don't work hard
This physical discipline was done to prepare us for our future employers
They will admire us for all the scars on our bodies and psyche
And we manage to stay alive
To serve them with a smile and sheer determination
No matter our health
Not even our humanity
All to get that seventy-five cents raise
We are the working-class men
And we should feel proud of our endurance"

And from "Stoopid":

"I wanted something else
Something that is terrifying
Horrifying
That would keep me up at night
Something that would make me want to crawl back into my mother's
womb
Even the devil himself would be petrified...
I want a tóxica!"

And from "Accent":

"My accent materialized on 84th Place
Between Wall and Main
It moves with the urgency of trying to get home before the sun comes
down
It moves like a paranoid criminal
Thinking it's going to get killed any minute
Any second
By a bystander"

When you read *Pimping My Trauma*, I recommended you read it with a
prayer for courage and a sense of humor. This is not a meek collection. It
is thick and it can pack a punch, even while making you laugh. So don't
power through it. Read it with tenderness and an open heart ready to dive
deep and heal. Our trauma does not have to bind us. Read these poems
with a liberatory intention. Your inner child will thank you.

If you are a trauma survivor, take care of you. If you or someone you
know is experiencing suicidal ideation, please reach out to the following
hotline - National Suicide and Crisis Lifeline: 988.

c/s
Brenda Vaca
Author of *Riot of Roses: Poems*
Founder, Riot of Roses Publishing House

Preface

I wrote this book for me
So you can read
And know what made me a me
Maybe you'll see yourself in me
Or remind you of someone that is like me
Perhaps there's many people like me
But don't want to admit it because it is embarrassing
Whatever the case it may be
The book was written for me to be free

I. Hi

Juan

My name is Juan
It rhymes with number one
Makes sense since I was the only one born in the hospital on
A lonely day
That number mocks me
I've been told "You are one weird muthafucka"

That number is associated with the highest rank of
Achievement
Like 1st place
To me it puts me in a strange place
In a different hemisphere

Juan is a lonely name like that lonely number
Juan was given to me after my father
Even he acknowledged my solitary lifestyle
"Yep, that one is going to fuck up my bloodline"

The funny thing is I've been called Juanito all my life
Juanito is a miniscule name for Juan
The smallness junior
I've always felt teensy-weensy
I was treated as such by my family

I can accomplish so much in life
Overcome bigger obstacles than my father
And they'll call me Juanito
I could conquer the world
Rule with an iron fist
Destroy cities
Choke slam a thousand-pound bear
Destroy universes and create new ones
Overthrow the kingdom of heaven
Summon Cthulhu and make him my bitch
And I can 110% guarantee you they'll still call me Juanito

Juan is a lonely name that rhymes with a lonely number
Juanito is a smaller name that is too small to rhyme with a number
Which is why I adopted a nickname
Given to me at age seven

BASEHEAD

It means crack addict
And I looked like a crackhead
I had a skinny-ass body
Dark bags under my eyes
Was so hyper that I climbed barbed wire fences
I stuttered
And lastly
I bit people
Hence the nickname Basehead

People from the hood called my name out of endearment
The joy and appreciation of calling me Basehead made me
Feel higher than number one
"THERE GOES THAT CRAZYASS BASEHEAD"
"MY N— BASEHEAD, who are you biting today?"

Basehead doesn't need numbers
Because they're always high
When baseheads do something crazy
Foos will always say
"Maaan that's one cracked out muthafucka I don't
Want to mess with"

II. Collapse

Super Duper Toxic Masculinity

He raised his son to be the big man
Made him watch porn
So his son knows
That a man fucks a woman
How a man fucks a woman
How a man dominates a woman

Just nine years old

Little big man cannot find a woman to fuck
He's too young
So he takes his sexual frustration out on his little friend

Just seven years old

Summer of '92
Childhood ended
Under a bright sun
Clear blue sky
And the birds were singing

The Clown

Twenty minutes, is all it took
To ruin this boy's future
He lost his power,
He lost his confidence
He lost his control for the next 16,830,720 minutes
Of his life
His family told him "Happy 39th Birthday. We love you"
But the boy didn't care
To him, birthdays make him question himself
"Why did I allow myself to get this far?"
"When am I going to end?" "How?"
"I shouldn't think about these thoughts.
My mom needs me to carry her to her last sleep.
But after that, what's going to happen to me?
What am I-"
"-Hey!"
The boy's thoughts are interrupted by his father
Demanding answers
"When are you going to bring a woman
To this house?
You're supposed to be married and
Have kids by now.
Do you like sucking dicks?
Come out of the fucking closet!"
But the boy won't answer him

He's too shameful to say the truth.

Thirty-two years of purgatory
Lost.
Confused.
He looks himself in the mirror, tells himself
"You don't deserve to have this body,
You don't know how to own it,
You're too paranoid to share it".

He tried to share his body before.
A woman told him that she wanted him inside of her.
Sexual acceptance
Is what the boy always desired,
Always daydreaming about
That woman was on his bed,
Waiting for him

But his memory from 16,830,720 minutes ago
Takes on this dark, humanoid form,
Covers the boy's mouth and squeezes his crotch,
And tells him "No, not now. Maybe never."
Now, see the confusion in her eyes,
See her dressing
And, finally, see her leave.
Just like the rest of them.
You're mine. Always remember that."

The boy–No...actually, he's no longer the boy,
The boy died at the age of seven, he pretended
To be a boy for the next five years.
After that, he pretended to be a teenage boy,
And now, he's pretending to be a man,
Which is funny because he likes to hide,
And he likes to be an entertainer,
To make others laugh and wonder–
His survival mechanism.

He is the clown.

A clown trapped in an abandoned circus.
Ask the clown "Why did you let yourself fall for those 20 minutes?"
And he will apply the boy's makeup,
And he will pour sour cream on the edges of his mouth,
He will look down on the ground,
And he will say,
"So they could let me play the Sega Genesis."

Never The End

My Little Bitch

I was birthed at the beginning of your downfall.
I became your stalker,
Dominating you whenever I could
No amount of pills and alcohol could take me
Away from you.
Sure, you can talk it over with someone,
But you better have an HMO plan
because I am your greatest expense.

I make you believe you can get rid of me
by falling in love.
My god,
Some bullshit hope you have.
I am the reason why you sleep alone every night.
I am the reason why you can't be touched
Sure, you can "use" me as an excuse
For why you won't let yourself be loved.
In return, I'll make you believe
That everyone is to blame.

And yes,
Suicide is bad,
But feeding on your life is gooooood.
The longer you live,
The bigger my belly gets,

And I will never explode.
You, however, will explode,
And everyone will know me.

But I am not all that bad.
I am the driving force of your creativity,
your imagination, your art.
I take you to different worlds.
I amplify the taste of food from different cultures.
I romanticize the aurora borealis,
something that you always wanted to see.
I heighten your senses when you are surrounded
By nature.
To take in the beauty this world has to offer,
I am convincing you that touching snow
Will be an epiphany.

I help you seek other artists that put their heart
And soul in their music,
So you can be put in a state of trance
By their melodies,
And then suffocate in your melancholy.

I hide you.

And I will keep on hiding you.
At the same time,
I put you on stage,
Make you feel free by talking about me.
And when people feel connected,

I raise your barriers
When they praise you,
I inject you with self-doubt.
Your "friends" will say
It is called "Imposter Syndrome,"
But that's not my name,
And they're not your friends,
You poor clown.

What is my name?

Let's see.
I do not have a physical form.
I am not your shadow.
I am darkly ethereal.
I can take any form and paralyze you with fear,
And you dreamt about me
Pursuing after you.
You were so close to home,
And you froze,
And you woke with shame,
Became guilt-ridden for the rest of the day.
Just like the other day,
Your niece could've died.
You tried to run after her,
But I stopped you.
So, you could see,
be a witness.
Sadly, for me
Nothing bad happened.

That could've been the most delicious meal
I would've eaten,
But
It's good to know that you can't protect anyone.
Perfect reason why you should continue to live
In your solitary confinement.

I think I've hurt you enough,
But remember this,
No matter how fast you can run,
No matter how strong you become,
No matter how smart you get,
I will always be there to tear you apart,
And make you start all over again.
And again...and again.

What's my name?
My name is Trauma.

And you will always be my little bitch.

The Day of

On the day of
Everything froze
Couldn't tell anyone
Because the outcome would be bad
Bloody
Forever leaving me feeling
Trapped
Indifferent
Uncertain
Untrue

I wonder if the same could be said
Of others like me

Grew up fast
Always felt old
Everyone around me grew
While I stayed the same
I felt abandoned by time
The syllabus of life no longer applied to me
The world is on fire but I can't feel the burn
The world is frozen but I can't see my breath
Happiness becomes my fear
Depression becomes my comfort
Love is distorted

Hate is clear
Yearning becomes exhausting before turning 19
Midlife crisis is laughable
Since I'm always in crisis
Daydreaming is my mental masturbation
Isolation is safe haven
Choose a passable behavior to cover my salvage mind
I keep myself hidden
I keep myself quiet
In need to make others happy
And in need for constant validation
To suppress this eternal violation

All of this traces back
To the day of

III. Broken Cherished Pieces

Mommy's Curls

I have my mommy's curls
They're beautiful
They're radiant
People love to tell me how healthy they look
They wish they had it like mine
They desire to feel it between their fingers
They want to brush it, play with it, and do cornrows
They want to be part of it

But I won't let them
Why?
Because they're all mine
And where did I get them from?
I got them from my mommy

People always ask me "What shampoo and conditioner do
You use?"
And I say "My mommy's love"

My mommy's curls are a threat to every guy's sexuality
They're not man enough to speak with their honesty
They always tell me, "Hey bro, your hair is-is-is tight"
"Tight? My hair is loose, it moves freely with the wind
You want to say that my hair is beautiful, but you can't
And I bet you wish your girlfriend had a hair like mine"

My mommy's curls are my force field on the dance floor,
To let everyone know not to mess with me when I'm synchronizing
with the beat of synthpop, EBM, goth and Italian disco
I use my mommy's curls to play with my baby nieces
By swaying my head left to the right
When they catch them
It becomes a tug of war
This trains their baby muscles
To prepare them for the world that is so abhorrent

This is my mommy's gift to me

It can also be a curse

My curls will carry on my mom's image, her wishes, and more
profoundly, her sorrow
From her painful memories
The memory of her mother beating her until she bled,
And yet, she still tries to make peace with her and takes the blame.
That's causes my curls distress.
The memory of my father betraying her love,
And yet, she remained with him to teach us forgiveness
That causes my curls to tangle into a painful knot
The memory of my brother denouncing her god and mocking
her faith
And yet, she's still trying to reason with him.
Hoping to see him by heaven's gate
That causes my curls to have split ends
The memory of my sister having an abortion
Her nightmare becoming a reality

Her breakdown
But she manage to get back up her feet
To love her and protect her
That causes my curls to fall and wonder what I did wrong
And other memories she has
That made her grow up so fast,
And she hides them

Just like I do

We know what those memories are made of
We know the dirt in our curls,
A silent acknowledgment between survivors

I have my mother's curls
They're not really curly
They are twisted and mangled
But she taught how me to treat them by applying a lot
of conditioner
To make them look healthy and shine
She also taught me the phrase that saves our faces from suspicion
and shame:
"There's nothing wrong with me, I'm okay,
I'm just a little tired. That's all"

Fat Boy

I loved my fatboy
I miss seeing that four-legged marshmallow
With his s'more-colored fur
Others saw him as just a backyard mutt,
But to me, he was still pure at heart

I would get ecstatic when he smiled
And wiggled his tail
I messed with his face
I gave him noogies
I wish he wore Fruit of the Loom underwear
So I could give him an atomic wedgie
I wish I could've hugged him tightly,
Just squeezed him until he popped,
But I didn't because it was not the right thing to do

But still,
Everytime when I pet him I would tell him
How much I would like to eat him
Throw him in a barbecue pit
Smoke him out

I had the urge to wrestle him
Every time I saw him sleeping
Peacefully on the ground

I imagined getting on top of the house
Doing an elbow drop on his fluffy stomach
Just to wake him up
Or

I would grab him by the throat,
And do a chokeslam to the center of the Earth
I would go celestial on him,
Pray to the cosmos to take form of a fist
And punch him directly
And I didn't care if it destroyed the world in the process
I just wanted to see my goal be accomplished

This is not toxic love
This is toxic cute aggression to the max
Thankfully for his sake, yours, and especially PETAs
Such violent desires never came to be

Even after he has been long gone
The thought of him still sends a violent rush
Through my chest
That overwhelms me,
And I submit myself to eternal regret
For not doing enough

This is my punishment for not taking him out
On walks, to the park or to the beach,
Or not letting him sleep in my room,
Those actions would be considered taboo
In my home
"He's just a fucking dog" I was always told

My Fat Boy was just a backyard mutt
And he still lives in the backyard of my mind

Emily

Have you seen her?
This girl with long black hair
And short bangs
She dresses all black
She has a heart shaped face
Sometimes wears cat ears
And she wear either
Chucks or Docs

Dammit
That could be any goth girl

Well she might look different now
Since it's been twenty years
But her name was Emily
Although her real name was Corrina
She called herself Emily
She named herself after the main character from
Emily the Strange comics
And she kinda looks like her too

Unlike other girls that wears dark get-up for aesthetics
She wears it to represent her inner turmoil
She was fucked up
She's a runaway

She had cops chasing after her at a backyard gig
Specifically looking for her

I called her to check if she was okay
But her foster parents picked up the phone
And asked me
"Have you seen her?
She hasn't been home for days
If you see her
Please tell her to come home"

When I asked my friends about her whereabouts
They scolded me
Telling me
"Stop giving a shit about her foo!
She's fucked up in her head
She's a slut
And she'll probably give you AIDS"

I tried to take that into consideration
Remembering when she told me
She does all kinds of drugs
Not only she injected herself with heroin
But with pure alcohol too
She playfully tells me
"I do it to hurt me more Juan
So I can feel everything"

People hated her
Girls beat the shit out of her

Because she slept with their boyfriends
Guys just used and abused her
But they all haven't seen her

I saw her differently
Because I suffer from the Messiah complex
"I can save her"
"I can fix her"
"I'm different from other guys because I treat her nice"
Every good guy's bullshit mantra

She didn't hide who she was
Unlike the rest of us
She didn't wear a mask
She wanted everyone to see that her humanity
Was bleeding
But she didn't know how to ask for help
To close her wound

She showed me an old photo of herself
Before she became Emily
She was Corrina
She was with her family
Didn't know which one
But they seemed happy
She had auburn hair, a yellow top, light blue jeans
And white shoes
It was a different feel
The other side of her that no one saw

She wasn't seen in my sexual fantasies
I tried but I couldn't
I just imagined holding her while she was in tears
As I sang along to "We're In This Together Now" by
Nine Inch Nails

That song that was playing on my headphones
After school
When I saw her walking from far away
She was wiping her face
As I read my friend's lips
Saying to me
"She got fucked up"

She disappeared through the parking lot gates

Then, she was gone

On the day she went missing
My brother was playing "Have You Seen Her" by
The Chi-Lites on his car
While we were merging onto the 110 North from
105 West Freeway
Gave me a better view of the city
Hoping that she was out there

A year later
To our surprise
We saw each other in a two-story house

Halloween party in Long Beach
She rushed and embraced me
She told everyone
"This is Juan!
He's my friend!
Don't mess with him!"
I blushed

The last image of her
Was when she was walking up the stairs
And she stopped
Looked at me
And smiled

She continued to ascend the stairs
To get her fix
So she could float with the stars

That was the last time I saw her

She called me later on
Told me was she was cleaned
Wanted to meet me to eat s'mores at
Roosevelt Park on Florence
I told her I'd let her know

But I never did

At that time
I was shielding me from everything

But I did not know
That would be the last time I heard her voice

Years later
I was told that she ODed

I felt numb
It was going to happen
I was told I couldn't save her early on
I didn't want to accept it
I tried
And I failed
She no longer exists

But she still exists on rainy days
Whenever I hear "The Rain Song" by Led Zeppelin
That song that I was listening to before I saw her
Again at the Halloween party
And reminds me that she was the first girl to walk
Me home on a rainy day
Halfway through
The rain stopped
And I could see the orange hues from the sun
Over the horizon
As I was listening to her innocent voice
We talked
Forgot what we talked about
But we communicated
We connected
There wasn't a quiet moment

She walked me to my house
Because she wanted to
The very first time I felt I wasn't a burden
We flowed like the stream on the sidewalk
That would eventually get drained in the sewage
But we kept on walking
Kept on talking
Until we said our goodbyes
She gave me a hug
Told me she'll see me around
She walked down on 84th place
And turned left on Main Street
Went on to get lost again

But somehow
I still see glimpses of her
I still think she's out there
Hoping that I'll reunite with an old friend to tell me
"I have seen her foo
I thought she was dead
But that was a lie
And she's doing alright
She takes the stairs every night
To kiss her child good night"

I will tell myself
"She finally made it"

A hopeless fantasy
To suppress the heartbreaking reality

She was just a girl

Just a girl

Whose first words to my shy younger self was

"Hi Juan, my name is Emily"

Echoes of Time

I am tracing back the echoes
From a distant past
I'm hearing laughter
Through the wavelength
Emitting from this photo

It has my brother
My cousins
And me
All hurled up on the lawn
To take this picture
Under the night sky

But now
We forgot the picture was taken
We forgot it existed
We even forgot that moment existed

I hear melodic music
That makes me see our youthful ghosts
On the lawn

I'm standing there
Hoping to interact with me
But they keep fading away

"Hey, are you okay?" my sister asked
"Just remembering" I said
"And I want it back
For it was the only time I felt joy
Without fearing the future"

IV. Floating

Girl at the Book Cafe

I keep coming to the same spot
Looking for a resolution
I keep walking away with no absolution

I saw a girl
Pale complexion
Dressed darkly
Dark hair with blonde highlights
Reading a book
Who looked like Susan Ballion of Siouxsie and The Banshees
I told her she looked lovely
She blushed and she thanked me
I walked away without asking for her name
I had to go to the Echoplex
And I was running late
Thinking I'll see her again
Thinking she's a regular at this place called Stories And Books Cafe

But Coronavirus hit
Put a pause on any possible interactions
Frustration arose
Regret took over

"If only I"
I ask myself that everyday

I could have talked to her
I could have gotten to know her
Shared music with her
Facetimed with her
Felt the thrilling sensation of meeting her outside
Under the lockdown
Trusted each other enough to be in each other's bubbles
Face to face.

"If only I"

I just saw her as someone who looked lovely
That was it
But she became an idea
An obsession
The "vaccine" for my loneliness

She became an object

If I approached her again
It wouldn't be for a genuine connection
Just a forced absolution
Through a superficial resolution

Valentine

Valentine's day
Twenty-four hours of
Anguish
Depression
Envy
Rage
Self-loathing
Shame

One particular summer night
Took the form of a woman

In an underground club
In a private dark room
She ordered me to take off my shirt,
Place myself onto the X-cross

So I did
She locked my wrists
So I wouldn't escape

Then she began to whip

Each hit
My muscles tightened
It hurt
But I wanted to hurt even more
I wanted to reach my limit

She'd pause
Checking if I was alright
As she caressed my back
Reminding me to give her a peace sign to stop

She continued

Despite her power
She was kind
Unlike my father
Who I had to hide from his rageful eyes

Hoping the physical discipline of the past would disappear
No longer did I have to hide the marks of the belt
Nor tighten my body when he was near
Hoping this consent will somehow make me heal
As she was erasing the turbulent traces of my back
With her soft fingertips
And felt her warm breath
Blowing on my invincible wounds

My back no longer flinched

It gave in
I began to feel comfortably numb

Then she stopped for good

I thanked her
Asked for her name
She said
"My name is Valentine
Now go buy me a water, bitch"

And I said
"Yes, ma'am."

21st Century Digital Love

I want to be seen
I want you to know that it is me
I want to be seen by you
Hoping that you'll say something to me
Hoping the stars will be aligned with you and me

I want you to see
The real me
What I wish to be
Hoping that you'll appreciate me

I want my happiness to be seen
I want my anger to be seen
I want my sadness to be seen
I want my hopes to be seen
So you can understand what makes me a me

But I'm tired of this being done digitally
Having fantasies where our eyes will meet
And our hearts will connect like rice and black beans

But alas,
My messages are seen
My being is left unseen

Chisme

I love being a metiche
I want to know who
Where
Como
Y porque

I just want to know!

I neeeed to know!

It's the only time where I can say
"Vaaaaalgame dioooos"
Or
"Y sabes que"
And my personal favorite
"No diiigas eeesooooo"

I wanna be up in people's business
Shit I'll stick my nose real deep
To smell that cheese
Good or bad
I don't give a fuuuck
Sin verguenza

All you foos thinking
"If that foo gets in my business
I'll fuck him up
Shit I'll break his nose!"

Please
You know that deep down
You are as exactly like me

When the chisme is that good
You wanna know
You have to know
You even fantasized being in part of the chisme
You wanna be the problem solver
The diplomat
The hero of the story
You wanna be praised for ending the bullshit

All the shit talking about our "TIAS" being chismosas
We became like them
We don't want to admit it
It's an evolution

That's why we use social media
We want to know what everyone's up to
And then pretend like we didn't see it
To make the story feel fresh

I love being a chismoso
People's lives fascinates me
It's thrilling
It's an ongoing story that you cannot fast forward
You got to wait

Especially with those that has court dates
That cheese is real good

Also it could be fucked up
Makes you wish you really want to do something about it
Out of good intentions
Not seeking rewards
But you can't
You cannot get involved
It goes against social norms
All you can do is see a train wreck slowly going off the rails
And it hurts to see one of the passengers is your loved one
You just hope for a divine intervention
That's all you can do
It's a freaking circus

The other downside of being a chismoso
Is not having a story for yourself
No one will tell your story
Because you're too busy reading someone else's
For that reason
You don't have a life
Nobody will know your name, your trials and
your accomplishments

If you are a subject of the chisme
Then congratulations
You have a life
Just make sure the cheese is that good
That's it has a positive ending
That inspires other chismosos like myself say
"Shit, fuck everybody. I gotta do what I gotta do. I don't care if it
makes me look bad. This is my life. I have choices. I'm gonna live
it. Now, get out of my way. I am going to take a huge slice of that
wedding cake, and tell the bride "Mija! Drop this foo! This foo is
un tóxico!"

You wanna know why this "angelic" groom
Es un tóxico?
Ask his best friend's wife
She was a part of it
Part of what?
I am not gonna say
I am done with that bullshit

I'm just gonna sit down
Eat this cake con un cafecito
And watch the chaos unfold

Stoopid

I'm stoopid
I thought I wanted a good girl
That would treat me nice
Telling me she loves me everytime
Makes dinner for me
That would caress my head when I'm feeling down
That would be loyal to me
That would always be there when I needed her

I would get mad when I would hear the statement
"Good girls only want bad boys"
I hated that
And I would told myself
"This is unfair!
I'm good guy,
I'm nice,
I'm very respectful,
I deserve a good girl,
I earn them,
They should want me,
They owe it to me,
It's logic"

When I spoke and heard myself saying that
I realized my heart was not in the right place
In fact
I felt like I was lying to myself

I wanted something else
Something that is terrifying
Horrifying
That would keep me up at night
Something that would make me want to crawl back into my
mother's womb
Even the devil himself would be petrified

And that is also fun

I want a tóxica!

That's what I want
And I know that's wrong
But I can't help it
I even feel naughty admitting it

I don't want a good girl that will make me a cake
On my birthday
I want a bad girl that will go missing on my birthday
Telling me "I was at my friends house
I forgot it was your birthday
Sorry "

I don't want a girl that will reply to my messages right away
I want a girl that will reply to it TEN hours late

I don't want a girl that will call me telling me
"Can you please pick me up?
My car stopped working
And I'm stuck on the freeway"
I want a girl who will call me at FOUR in the morning
Telling me
"Hey, pick me up
I'm in Moreno Valley,
I'm at a party,
I thought I invited you.
I guess I forgot.
Sorry. Tee hee hee hee"

I'm stoopid because I want her
And I want her because I'm stoopid

I know some of you guys are thinking
"You don't want that shit, bro
Trust me it's not worth it
Save yourself pinche estoopid"
I'll say to you
Let me have the experience
I want to know what it's about
I want to be part of fun and feel the thrill
I want to clash with the negative energy
I want to get lost in the unknown
I want to taste the corruption

I want to be fused with chaos
So once the bullshit is over
You and I will go grab a beer
And talk about it
But if your stupidass orders us bottles of IPA
I will fucking stab you

Nastyass beers
For people who can't get over their nastyass exes

I want a tóxica that my mommy will not approve of
She'll plead with me:
"Deja de esa muchacha
Ella es hija de satanás!"
And I want my tóxica to tell me:
"If you listen to your mom,
Then I'm going to send her all the photos and videos
Of me doing things to you
And she will see that her little Angel
Is now my little Sucio"

I'm stoopid because I think I could fix her
And I think I could fix her because I'm stoopid

Now that I heard myself saying this
Maybe having a tóxica is not a good idea

It sounds hot
But I don't want to get myself burned
I have to be cool
So I won't have to be anybody's fool

Okay, I just recalibrated my desires

I want me a good girl
That will treat me nicely
Who acts nice to mommy
Who will feed me
Just as I feed her
And who will be there for me
Just as I am there for her

And every night
When we go to sleep
When I lay my head on her chest
She'll whisper sweetly into my ear
She'll say:

"I love you so much
You're my one and only
But
if you break my aching heart
I will fucking stab you

Goodnight stoopiiid"

Honda Civic 2018

I was born in 2018
With the newest technology
Sleek body design
Nice cushion seats
Better sound system
Giving you stress-free trips
With no engine light on

Yet
You still treat me like your old car
You haven't stopped by and asked me
"How are you doing?
Pop the hood off to check on your forehead"

You make me drive you on the same route
As your old car did
I could go further
I'm ready for it
It's not a problem
I'm more reliable
I can take you across the state
See places that neither of us have been to
Feel the temperature changes

If it rains I'll be your umbrella
If it gets scorching hot I'll be your AC
And I'll keep us moving

I can do that no problem
But you keep on making me drive
An eighteen-mile radius
I think to myself
"Is this really what I was made for? I was shipped across the ocean
to be circling around the same streets, same freeways?
This is depressing"

Is that what you are?
I don't want to be driven in blue
I am tired stopping for red
I want to keep going on green
Go as far as you and I can see

Heat

The heat suppresses my will to leave the couch
The sweat of my body became adhesive
The hours going by and I'm missing out
My selfish needs are at a pause
I can't even masturbate
Damn

I am thirsty for a fresh cold smoothie
Fresh coconuts from the street's vendors
The real heroes of the summer

I'm hoping to crawl into my bathtub
Fill it with cold water
Sleep until the air cools down

I must make the effort to step out
Live my day
Can't let something from 93 million miles away
Bring me down

How funny
So far and yet feels so close
Just like bad memories

Gravity

The clouds I wish I could reach
The stars I wish I could be
Constellations that yearn my soul to be free
The dirt reminding me that I cannot be
The wind tries to give me wings
The gravity holds me down
Says "you will never be"

Bands

I need to see them
Play their hearts out
Melodies they chose
As an extension of their humanity

I need to see them
See their expressions
Yearning anger resentment hope
Shaped by their instruments

I need to hear them
Hear their voice
Hear their beating hearts through drum
Hear their aura through guitars
Hear their foundation through bass

I need to feel them
Feel their notes
Feel their harmony and dissonance
Feel their soul

I need to be inspired by them
Guide me through my inner instruments
Find my own melodies
Compose my own symphony
Hoping that will inspire others like me

The Water

There is something in the water
There's no moon to make it move
No sun to shine its blue
Just the gray sky to let me know my end is nigh

There is something in the water
It's ominous
And yet
Still

There is something in the water
A melodic hymn is summoning for my insanity
To take a deep dive
It wants to bathe me with its depth of chaos

There's something in the water
I dip my hands in
And ...

There's nothing in the water

I'm just being a drunk

Romanticizing something that is not there

Yet
I wouldn't mind a siren calling for me
Pulled by her angelic voice
Drowned in her embraced

In Need of Freedom

I need to stop jerking off
I am tired of this shit
It has gone on for too long

First I did it out of discovery
That followed with shame
I used to think every time when I jerked off
Some fucked up shit was going to happen the next day
Like a "day after curse"
Be it family problems, 9/11, or my dog going missing
All because of my hand
...and I was raised catholic too
Which plays into the whole
guilt-driven afterthought

Eventually I started doing it without feeling guilty
Just for pleasure
It was pure bliss
A moment of relief
Just to feel free
I did it seven times a day
I was proud of my endurance
I was my own champion
I was my own escape

Some people said it takes them five minutes to do it
Fucking amateurs
It takes an hour!
God knows what goes on in their heads
But I am not about that bullshit
You have to think of a setting, the time, the senses, the wording
You have to visualize it
Once you create the art of it
Then you have to let yourself go into your own imagination
Most importantly
You have to engage with the person that you want to be in love with
Mentally, emotionally, psychologically
You have to blend those in or otherwise you'll be just wasting time
Think about the colors and the warmth
Once you and that person feel connected
Then that's when you have the sex
You need to savor each other's bodies
And when you two finally climax
That's when you cum in the real world
And that's why it takes an hour!

Five minutes–that's straight out bullshit!
The fuck is wrong with them

...Maybe they weren't abused as kids...

Well, that's too bad for them and too bad for their art
For 26 years
I have engaged in over one hundred relationships
...in my head of course...

Now that I finally grounded myself
Because of therapy
I lost the art of it
And I lost time
I realized it was an addiction
I just needed to feel good
I do wonder if it was harmful in some way
Now, when I do it
I just do it
Just to feel...something

I stand here before you
With shame and guilt all over again
In need of strength and cleansing
In need of forgiveness and encouragement

In need of freedom

Burnt

I am burned out
I keep repeating the same cycle
Wake up, jerk-off, go to work, go to the gym,
come back home, jerk-off again, and then,
worry about tomorrow
Hoping it'll be different
Frustrated that I didn't make a difference today
Defeated that it will happen again tomorrow and after that

I am burned out
I want to be drained
Just pass out and never wake up again

The Big Escape

I escaped South Central
Because I got tired of dodging bullets
And I was hurting my back and joints in doing so
If I was on a gymnastic team
I would've brought gold medals to this country
I would've been the "Greatest American Athlete"...
Until I did something fucked up
Then I'd be considered a Latino-American, Mexican-American or
South Central American

I escaped South Central
Because I got tired of blood getting on my clothes
That my mom bought for me from Mervyns
Also, I got tired of seeing death too
But the pants were very special to me
She got them 20% off by applying for credit

But now,
I live in Los Feliz
Beautiful place, peaceful, clean
I don't dodge bullets anymore
My clothes are always clean
All is quiet on the western front

But I can't sleep
I have to call bomb threats in my street
So the sound of sirens and helicopters can help me sleep
When I do
I sleep like a baby

I escaped South Central
But South Central won't escape me

Imagine Me

I want to be that person who I imagine being
But in reality
I'm struggling

I want to be that person who knows what he is doing
And knows where to go
But in reality
I'm confused

I want to be that person who is grounded and appreciates
Everything he has accomplished
But in reality
I'm floating

I want to be that person that has somebody to share everything
But in reality
I'm lonely

I want to be that person that a guy feels threatened by
Wondering if his girlfriend is sending me messages in the middle of
the night...or spooning
But in reality
I'm just jerking off to pictures of her on Instagram

I want to be that person who isn't afraid of the changes
that need to be made
In order to ascend
But in reality
My paranoia is making me descend into comfort
I want to be that person that my parents wish I could be
But in reality
They are as worried as I am

I want to be
But in reality
I just imagine and see

White Russian

Shall I compare you to a white russian
I feel joy and lightheaded
When I consume you
The buzz feeling makes me suspend gravity
Making me wish that you'll be a part of me for Infinity

You give me fear when you are not there completely
Whether there be no ice, milk, vodka or coffee liquor
My heart becomes an empty glass
Desperately trying to fill in the void

But once you are there completely
I consume you so much
Way beyond the limit
That I collapse to the ground

And I go to the gym
I do squats
I lift weights
I bench press
I can pick you up with my pinky and throw you across the room

But it's what makes you that weakens me
As I see you on the table above me
No matter how small you are seen
You have enough power and proof to destroy me

My World in their Eyes

The state of the world has aligned with my world
People desperately trying to have physical contact
Finding an excuse to be outside
Don't want to be boxed in a mental prison,
But I'm used to it
As a matter of fact
I became a master of it

I tell them "Hey, you'll be fine. Just pick a hobby"
But I lied
People's desperation has aligned with my desperation
Their frustration has aligned with my frustration
Their isolation has aligned with my isolation

For the first time ever
I saw my world being televised
It is no longer in my head, it is on the streets
On their faces
And I want to destroy it
I'm tired of it

Kill the wishful thinking
That somebody will do it for me
Realized the bed I saw as a sanctuary is actually
A part of my own mental prison cell

Burn the memories that paralyzed me
Half of my lifetime
Break down the door that kept me locked in
Start to have faith in myself and trust it
Most importantly, have the courage to do it
And do it now

Ghost Dancer

You see him on the dancefloor
Whether it is a club or a bar
He's there
There's no one around him

You see his head bopping to the punching bass
His arms moving with the patterns of synthesizers
His feet synchronizing with the beat
His arms swooning with the melody

The fog machine and darkness embraces him
Making him feel safe
Whereas the blue and purple lighting highlights his
Sexual ambiguity

Again there's no one around him
He's by himself
He's dancing by and to himself
He's a ghost dancer

He was first seen dancing to Indie Pop at
Club Par Avion in Radisson Hotel on East Hollywood
Then dancing to 80's at Club AM/FM in
Grand Star Jazz Club on Chinatown
Synthpop and Coldwave at

Club Mode:M in Monte Cristo in Koreatown
Industrial and Agro-tech at
The Batcave at Medusa Lounge in Filipino Town
Chicago House and Afro House at
Warehouse LA in Los Globos in Silverlake
Hi-NRG and Rock en Español at
Chulita Vinyl Club in La Cita in Downtown LA
and Darkwave at Dark Disco in
Footsies in Highland Park

Anything with a groove
He busts his moves
Except for reggaeton and rap
Those two styles don't sync with his need of expression
And he feels ashamed
He was raised on the streets where rap gave it an identity
A name that nobody should fuck with: South Central
He wants to have pride of the cracked cement he walked on
But can't synchronize with the music that was blasted
Because it's not chaotic
It is structured like reggaeton, cumbia and salsa
And they required a partner

Ghost dancers don't have partners
They are conductors of strange activities
He uses his hands to conduct a story
A strange activity for everyone to see
He only exists in his own celestial plane
He used to be desperate for someone to join him
But it's no longer a necessity

His frequency has become unmatched

He dances with the ghosts of those he wished he loved
He tries to outdance the demons that haunts him

When someone joins him
It becomes a threat
Not the welcome he had hoped for

But make no poor assumptions
His moves are good
No they're excellent
A guy told him so when he was dancing to Boy Harsher
The slowness synth heavy beat
That goes from sexual regression to sexual oblivion
That's his style
Guy said he was trying to keep up with him
If a guy couldn't keep up with him
Then what chance does a woman have?
That's what frustrates him
Can he outdance a ballerina or does he want to
Slow dance with her?

Doggy style and perreo are his kryptonite
It doesn't call for his pain
It demands submission to social norms
It doesn't request a story that his body can articulate
It forces him to pelvic thrusting against his comfort
In so he denies
He walks through the bodies on the dance floor

They don't need him
And he doesn't need their mediocrity
Fuck them

Now he is on the bus as the prelude to his solo
Performance
He gets home
Into his mental cell
And he calls for an orchestra
He plays Drain by Whirr
A shoegaze song to harmonize the dissonance of his isolation
He starts by laying catatonic
At the 2:20 mark
He slow dances on his own
With every snare that hits
Feels like it is punishing his regrets and his mental suppression
At the 3:51 mark
That's when his spirit suspends
And gravity cannot suppress him
He is levitating on his own
He imagines an acceptable life
Where others will be happy for him
Happiness becomes a reality for just those minutes
In realty
He's a mime
With his hands conducting his soul for satisfaction

This is the ghost dancer's way

Ghost dancers are not ruled by any social laws
They don't fall under any criteria
And they all have different stories
Do not pity them, condone them, or condemn them
Or even try to empathize with them
Ghost dancers will sway through your
Understanding
And forever be astronomical
Above your humanity

Until the music stops

Move

I want you to move for yourself
But not with your booty
With your soul

I wanna see how a song really makes you feel
Not just the chorus
But the very beginning of a note
I wanna see you dance to a sad song
How you express your pain
But not from a former lover
That's overdone
Just being alive in this world

What song sets you free
That's not on the Top 40 Hits
What are the frequencies that tunes in with your celestial being?
The decibel that your heart beats?
What song makes you yearn to be free?
What song makes you flip the bird for everyone to see?
What song makes you be what you wish to be?
What song makes you wish everyone could see?

I want to dance with you
But I don't want to be the only peacock on the dance floor
Your two step is not enough for me

I wanna see you take control on the dance floor
Challenge me
I wanna see every girl being jealous
While their boyfriends are in awe

I want you to break my heart
But not just mine
Everyone's
So we can remember a life form moving in different shapes
Moving with the rhythm of the beat
Morphing with the melodies

I wanna be filled with pessimism
Thinking I'll never have you
Which will give off the regret
Of not even trying to reach you
I'll make excuses
Lies even
Saying "I'm too much for you"
"I'm too busy"
"It was not meant to be"
"It'll never work since I got issues that needs to be fixed"

But what I really want
Is to surrender to you
Kneel before you
Collapse before you
Into a thousand pieces
So you can kick some of it
Telling me

"Hey come on,
don't give up on me,
put yourself back together.
The song is about to end"

I don't know what this is
It's not S&M
It's something indescribable
Don't want to put you on the pedestal
It's overdone

I just want something that is majestic
Something that the planets and stars will align
And other cheesy cosmic romance shit

I want to be equal with you
And yet
I want the both of us to feel special
I want us to blend in with the red and purple lighting
Under the disco ball

So throw that cocktail away
That could be replicated any other day
Our energies space and time cannot
Our presence is not guaranteed for a second chance
Iris by Pastel Ghost is playing
And the climax is about to hit

Let's move into something that is completely human
Let's move into something that is heavenly ethereal
Let's move into something that is everlasting
Let's move into something that will forever be our reverie

Do It

I'm wasting my goddamn time masturbating to these models
on Instagram
As sickening as it sounds
I find solace that I graduated from jerking off to hentai

These Instagram models
I don't know what they're about
They all strike the same pose
Go to the same festivals

I pleasure myself because I need an outlet
I tried with piano
Collecting movies in 4K
Traveling
Almost died in Transylvania
Clubbing

But it all goes back to
The bed
And the workplace restroom
Forty-minute tops
So I can immerse myself into my thoughts
Just to escape

The dance floor is no longer my refuge
I didn't want to admit it
But I have to face the music

Maybe I should cut my penis off
That will stop the shameful act
At the same time
I won't know the pleasure of coupling with someone

Perhaps connecting with someone will stop it
But that will prove the old bastards with
their old ways of thinking right

I can no longer run from sex
But I don't want to force myself to do it
I just want a guaranteed positive experience from it
But I'm tired of playing the game to get it
I don't want myself or the other person get hurt by it
But I have to get on with it
I don't like that abuse has hindered me from experiencing it
But I'm tired of getting frustrated from it

I need to do it

Just to end it
Just to get something from it

My Room

My room has four walls.
They're white.
It could be an asylum
And that's all right.

It has a TV,
Which I hardly watch,
It has a bed
Where I spend most of the day.
It has a love couch,
But it's empty.

My room is empty.

I imagine it has life,
It has people,
It has music playing,
Hearing laughter from a corner,

Having loved ones,

But I see other things.

I see the white walls abstract,
Something dreadful,
Waking up to see the walls covered in organic flesh,
See my body painfully fused with it,
Becoming a living, grotesque mural
That breathes out an agonizing mechanical sound.

My face, the center of it,
Strained and distorted.

That's what I see
When I feel disassociated from humanity,
From my humanity as well.

What I really want to see
Is green,
But not just any green.
I'm talking about...mystical green,
Spring green,
Rainforest green,
Or Seafoam green,
Like the sea.
Yes, I like the sea.

I could smell the salty sand.
I could hear the waves.
I could feel the warmth from the sun and cool
Breeze.
I could taste the seaweed.
I could see where I want to be
At peace.

My room will no longer be seen as a prison.

It will be seen as a place for me to dream.

Snooze

I turn off my alarm clock
because I got tired of waking up to it in the morning
I was waking up to a mechanical sound
To an empty void
That dictated my day

I was not waking up to see a smile
Or a life form
Or the smell of pancakes
Or the sounds of bacon grizzling
Or the smell of the aroma of coffee
I was not waking up to humanity
I was waking up to machine

I hated Mondays
If Monday was a person
I'd beat the shit out of it
I'd even torture it
Beyond recognition
And deep down in your darkest desires
You'll turn a blind eye and wouldn't mind

But I decided to take a step back

And asked Monday

"How do you feel about being the most hated day of the week?
It told me
"I feel bad
I don't make you hate me
They make you hate me
I am the start of a new week
That should inspire you to try something new

My name is known in many languages as
Moon Day
I was named after the moon
A satellite
That you can look up to
Get inspired by
You can romanticize it
In return
It'll provide you the light when you're surrounded by darkness

And in some religions
I am the start of fasting

But your employer took all that away from me
And they made you their bitch
And you blame me for it?

Do I order you to wake up at six-thirty in the morning?
Do I release you at five in the evening?
Do I box you in your car for three hours?
Who is telling you that I'm not allowing you
To go to the beach in the middle of the day?

Who is telling you that I'm not allowing you
To focus on yourself?
Who is telling you that I'm not allowing you
To have time for yourself?
Who is telling you all this shit?

If a loved one accomplishes their dream,
Do you have to seek me for permission to celebrate
With them?
If a loved one is yearning for you,
Do you have to seek me for permission to be with them?
Because if it was up to me,
I'll give you all the time you want or need,
Not just two weeks.
If a loved one dies, do you have to seek me
For permission to mourn?

Do you have to seek me for permission to be
A human being?

I never made any rules
Your masters did
But you need them because you got bills to pay
And gas prices are going up!
Milk and eggs too!
But I am not the one jacking up the prices

What's funny is that there's millions of you
And few of your bosses
You can overthrow them
But they got you brainwashed into thinking that any
Positive change will be the end of you
You are their slave to the wage
But you know this already
And you still take it out on me?!
So instead of asking me how does it feel
To be the most hated day of the week,
How about if I ask you
"How it feels to be the most miserable,
Piece of shit, punkass-bitchass-coward
In your little cubicle?
If you can't answer that
Just hit the snooze button
Because that's all you're going to be doing
For the rest of your life"

The next morning
I get in my car
And Tuesday asked me
"After all that Monday told you,
You're still doing the same thing?
That's sad"

Air

The smog in my city fogs my mind and my vision
Until I breathe in what Mother Nature meant to giveth
Air
So crisp and clean
Like pouring ice cold Sprite into my nose
This is a gift from one of Mother Nature's favorite saints
Santa Cruz
Feeling the green that is not artificial
Smelling the wood that is not a pencil
Smelling Earth
That cleanses my mind and puts aside my
Corrupted memories
Gone was the sound of babies crying
Gone was the sound of mothers wailing over their
Dead children on the streets
Gone was the sound of gunshots and helicopters
Gone was the sight of concrete with washed out blood
Gone was the sight of decomposed veterans and
Dreamers that never reach their full potential
Gone was the sight of my abuser, with the lingering
Question "When?"
Gone was the sight and feeling of my father's disappointment
and rage
Gone was the sight and feeling of my mother's desperation
and sorrow

Gone was the imagination of my own purification by
Having a javelin descending from the sky
Piercing into my heart and slowly twisting it to spew
Toxins that hinder my growth
All that shit was gone
I exhale Death
And I inhale Life
I heard the sound of leaves falling gently on the ground
I heard and felt the wind passing by
From far away I heard the waves from the ocean
Dancing with each other
I heard birds
Lots of them
I saw the greenest of the green
And the brownest of the brown on the ground
I saw the bluest of the blue
And the whitest of the white in the sky
I saw clarity
A clearer vision
But most importantly, I felt the sun's radiance
It's warmth gave me comfort
For the first time, I felt peace
And I told myself, "If only I can always feel like this,
If only I could go to sleep feeling like this"

V. Frustrations

A Catholic Haiku

I am Catholic
I'm always guilty of shit
Drown me in whiskey

Little Dude (Little Boy pt.1)

Little Dude fucked up my weekend
I told him "We're going out to have some fun"
He told me "Nah, I wanna stay in bed"
"Come on peepee, fuck the bed!
We're going out, whether you like it or not"
"Ah man, not this again" he said

At the Grand Star Jazz Club,
I was flirting with a girl.
I made her laugh.
I told Little Dude,
"Little Dude, we have potential."
Then little dude asked me,
"Do you think she'll love me?"
"Little Dude don't worry about that shit bro,
just go with the flow, mijo.
We'll be fine"
"I'll try." he said.
 He always says.

On the dance floor,
She started grinding on me,
But little dude started with his bullshit:
"I can't breathe," he said.
"Fuck your breathing, put your CPAP mask on!"

"I don't wear that, you do."
"Fuuuck, hold it for at least two more songs."
"Tell her to stop!"
We wrestled.
The girl left.
"Little Dude you fucked it up again"
He remained quiet
"Ah fuck it, let's get food."

Halloween night 2021,
I promised little dude that we'd keep to ourselves
And that I'd respect his...space.
But I met someone.
She asked for my phone number.
I gave it to her.
I walked away in glee.
What's more, I heard her say to her friend,
            "you see, I told you I'd get his
            phone number."
Little Dude and I became happy.
First time that ever happened.

Date night,
We were spooning on her couch.
We started making out.
Then
She opened her legs,
Invited Little Dude to go inside.
"Little Dude, she wants you inside...her house."
"I'm not ready"

"Little Dude, we've gone this far."
"This is too soon."
"Ah, fuck this."
I grabbed Little Dude by the throat
To put him inside.

But he became heavy
And I became too weak to carry him
I was dragging ourselves to go inside.
The woman asked me,
       "Are you okay?"
"Yes, I am."
       "If you feel like your Little Dude
       can't go inside-"
I interrupted her.
"I can do this-I can do this."
Then she said,
       "You can't force your Little
       Dude if he doesn't want to.
       It's not good for the both of us."
She had a point.

I started to explain to her
"Sorry, I think...Little Dude wants to know you first."
       "He wants to trust me."
"Yeah"
       "Because he has been hurt."

How did she know that?
"Yeah, it happened a long time, 29 years ago to be exact.
I was a little boy, but he doesn't let that go."
        "I've been hurt too," she said.
        "I know what that's like. I'll
        Wait until he feels both safe
        And comfortable."
Something about that made me see Little Dude differently.
"Yeah, he does want that."

For a whole month
We've been on her porch.
We tried to lure him in.
"Little Dude, she's not shaming us. She is
Compatible, it's ok for you to go inside."
"I'm trying, I'm really trying."

On Wednesday, December 1st
Little Dude stepped his foot in the doorway.
The woman and I got excited.
"This is it. Just one more step, man, you're in.
Now we know what it feels like."
But Little Dude stopped
And gave me the thousand-yard stare,
Asking me,
"Are you using me or are you using her?"

I was lost for words.
Little Dude slowly walked back outside to the porch.
He wrapped his arms around the gate,
Looking lost
Just like the day he was left undone.

Saturday morning
The woman told me,
        "I'm sorry, I can't keep this
        Door open. It's getting cold,
        And it's getting lonely. I need
        To be warm and I need to be
        In love. I cannot wait anymore."
"I understand. I'm hoping that you'll be the last person
To tell me that."
We tried to smile for Little Dude's hopeful future,
but our frowns overwhelmed us.
We both knew that the optimism was a lie.

        "Your Little Dude needs to talk
        to someone."
"He does, but I'm not sure how long it's going to take."
Little Dude and I left.

Walking down the street
Are so many houses that I wish Little Dude
And I could've visited.
Some are haunted with ghosts.
One where I was going to be their first visitor,
I thought Little Dude was going to feel secure there,

But he decided to go home,
And the doors kept closing.
Why try? I always wondered.
Soon there'll be no doors opened.
The ones that'll be opened will be like a shelter.

Little Dude,
What should I do with you?
And what should you do with me?
We both want to lie under the sun.
Do we have to get hurt again so the pain will make
Us go inside a house?
Because we can't find the love that we both want that way.
It's not good for us.
What should we do?
I'm tired of being in bed,
Imagining going in houses.
I'm tired.
I'm so...so...tired.
Speak to me.

And so, he did.

"I'm small.
I'm scared.
I'm stuck.
I'm lost.
I can't make them feel what they want to feel.
I can try,
But it's a lie.

I cannot be who they want me to be.
I can pretend but it's a lie.
They cannot be who I want them to be.
They can pretend but it's still a lie.
Since I cannot be who I want to be,
I cannot make them happy if I'm not happy.
What scares me the most is that
I'll be the one that'll burn their house down.
If I do,
Then what will be the point of feeling so small all this time?
I need pain
Because pain is all that I ever knew.
It groomed me.
It's real.
I need to be punished.
If they cannot punish me,
Then solitary is my punishment.
And it's ok."

I realized I was not talking to the Little Dude anymore.
I was talking to the source
Our everlasting virus

The Little Boy.

Kill the Little Boy (Little Boy pt.2)

Momma
I'm going to kill my Little Boy
He's been dragging me down
He doesn't let me go
He keeps reminding me of the shit I went through
He scares me
He paralyzes me
He convinces me that others have a worst
Perception of me
I don't want him around anymore
He doesn't let me grow
He keeps hiding the control
He keeps tying my feet
He keeps locking me in my own room
He keeps pushing others away
He bullies me
He calls me "little bitch" all the time even when I'm
Eating with you
He doesn't let me feel proud of my
Accomplishments
Always says "there's somebody always better than
You"
He doesn't let me be honest
He doesn't let me have what I want
He doesn't let me sleep peacefully

He's the reason why I'm tired all the time
I think he is the reason why I use the
CPAP machine

When I see something wrong he holds me down
Telling me "let it fall"
He doesn't let me experience love
My friend told me to give him love
My therapist told me to make peace with him
But I don't want to
I've been his bitch for the last 30 years
He doesn't deserve love or peace
He deserves to die
That's why I'm going to kill him
So I can be free
That's what I am going to do to my Little Boy, Momma
I'm gonna kill him

And I wish you can do the same thing to your Little Girl

Insomnia

Can't sleep
Tossing and turning
I'm losing my mind
Thinking death has already claimed me
I just have come in terms with it
I'm paranoid
I jerked off thinking it will help me
It did not since I'm writing this down at 3:57 am
I need to sleep now so I can wake up in 3 hours
To go to work
Fucking bills
Drank 96 proof alcohol
But got my mind racing at 96 mph
Maybe I need to bury myself in a woman's breasts
But that's a long journey to achieve
I can cut short with money, but I'll feel cheap
The CPAP machine is not helping
Hours that I lost will soon catch up
Looking forward to collapsing in a public place
Perhaps become narcoleptic
It's now 3:58am
I'm overthinking
I'm being stupid
I just need more alcohol
Maybe 5 shots of whiskey

Or absinthe
Perhaps this time I'll die of alcohol poisoning
Whatever it takes
I need to fucking sleep
Even if it means for an eternity

Chi-chis

I have a mental disease
Which causes me to have this repulsive need,
To lay my head on your chest
And suck on your breast

I want to bury my head into your heart
Because I want to feel safe
In a feminine space
Because my space is isolated and cold
And the Little Boy in me is looking for a home

I know you'll say
"I don't want to deal with this bullshit again
I won't be your mommy, boy
You should go back home
Until you're fully grown"

How I wish the Little Boy would free himself from
Trauma
So I wouldn't be looking around to see who will be
My momma
I'm tired of crawling around on my knees
Pleading with you
And this distorted need to be under your responsibility

I don't want my mommy
I want you
I just want to feel what is like to be with another
Who is not my mother

But still feel secure
So I will no longer have to look for the cure
Still feel warm
Like not feeling the cold by drinking all the rum
Still feel calm
Like the palm trees that rest easy under the sun
Still feel the embrace
In hoping the disease can be erased

So I can sleep at night at ease
Breathing all air that I need
Without the need of that CPAP machine

So I can stop drinking at night
To erase this humiliating thought
That I need to be under childcare

I want to inhale your breasts
The foundation of your body that feeds life

I wish I didn't have this age regression
So my life would have a natural progression

But my infant needs have taken over me
Preventing me to be
Who you need me to be

Is this Kink?

During my "self-pleasure zone" hours
My fantasies can be...unorthodox
Hands tied, kneeled, beaten down to submission
By a woman...red-head preferably
My mind is telling me:
"She'll love you more,
If you let her dominate you"

I always imagine seeing her smiling face
When she's on top of me
Her hands on my throat
Whispering into my ear
"You're my favorite toy"
While my mind is telling me:
"She'll appreciate you more,
If you let her play you"

I always imagine seeing the joy on her face
As she swings her whip
Peeling my skin
While my mind is telling me
"She'll cherish you more
If you let her enslave you"

I always imagine her
Walking me around on a leash
Petting me
Telling me how much she loves me
While my mind is telling me
"She'll embrace you more
If you let her humiliate you"

I imagine kneeling before her
Caressing my cheek
Playfully bopping my nose
Then proceed to dehumanize me
By urinating and vomiting on me
While my mind is telling me
"She'll care for you more,
If you let her break you"

I imagine she would tell me in tears
How much she wants to break me
Forcing me to see her body being ravaged
By her other lovers
Telling me she loves me so much
That she wants to destroy me
While my mind is telling
"She'll love you forever
If you let her destroy you"

Then I start to wonder
Is this really kink?
Am I really convincing myself

This is the type of pleasure I want?
Am I convincing myself
This is the most selfless act I can do?
Just to be loved?
Am I convincing myself
This will help me erase the harm that was done?
By replacing the forces that broke me
With feminine figures
That I desire to be engage with
It's okay, right?

This is sexual healing, right?
Or
Punishment?
Maybe I need her dominance
Her violence
Her evil eye
So I can feel comfortable
Move freely in chaos

Maybe I should not romanticize or sexualize
My degradation
It's wrong
But I am convincing myself
That's the only way I can feel right

Am I stuck in a cycle?
Is this really kink?

Dread

I want to talk to you
Because I want to know you
I want to be with you
Because I want to fall in love with you
But I need to approach you first
And I don't know how

I don't want to be an intruder
How can I make your face look from alarming to amusing?

Maybe I should relax myself
Tell myself
"You are not a dickwad
You are not a monster
You are not going to hurt her
Stop with these bullshit thoughts
Stop being afraid"

But why this fear?
Where did it come from?

Ah shit
I'm freezing now
Not this again

Now I'm recalling those stories that I've heard
When I was young
And it always ends with the phrase
"That's life"

When I tell the storytellers how much it affected me
They're puzzled
Telling me
"Don't feel that way
It didn't happen to us
You're easily traumatized"

They're right
But I also think that it's wrong
That a ten year old boy
Hears a story
where a husband penetrated his wife with a shotgun
And well...

She survived
But she can't have children
Like she wanted to

I thought these stories were meant
To build my mental endurance
But I was wrong
It didn't made me tough
It made me numb
It made me accept that the world is fucked up
And there's nothing I can do about

And I cannot complain
Because it hasn't happened to my mom
And my sisters

My mind tells me
"Maybe one day it will
You'll never know"
My mind always scared me
Into thinking that
I might be the one with the shotgun
Since I was ten years old
With those thoughts
Amplified it with my abuse
An event that left me confused

But I cannot tell you about it
Because you'll turn away
And I'll understand
At least I was being honest
And yet be wrong in doing so
Which is something I'm very good at
I'm always doing something wrong
Even when I know I'm doing nothing wrong
I convince myself that I'm doing something wrong
Because I'm doing nothing
I'm letting everything that is wrong happens
And anxiety attacks come to play
When there's no one around to make me feel okay
I have to call my sister on the phone
So I won't deal with episode on my own

As I'll lament on the lessons
that were given to me to survive

"Do not get involved
It's not your problem
Keep your mouth shut,
Keep your head down
If you hear someone screaming in the alley,
Don't answer
Don't be a hero
And don't look for a hero
If you do,
It'll be your turn to scream
So stay silent,
And you'll make it out alive"

I took those guidelines
To block out any responsibility
For humanity
But now
It makes me freeze
I cannot fight or flee
Just stand there and let it happen
But the worse thing of all
I just want to see how much it affects me
I want to see how much it kills me
A dark twisted desire
To feed my shame
To feed my pain
because I am a coward

I was molded to become one
In order to survive

Yes

I am survivalist too

I have to do and not do things to survive

That makes me intelligent
And yet
Still in the wrong

Why am I thinking about this?
What the fuck is wrong with me?
I'm in a cafe shop
I'm waiting for my coffee
I have my sweet bread
It's a honey cookie bread from an Armenian bakery
It's quiet
There's no crime happening
My surroundings are clear
So what the fuck triggered these thoughts?

Maybe it's the fear that I have
that I cannot provide anything to you
I cannot please you
I cannot shelter you
I cannot protect you

And what is it I want you to provide me?
Healing?
Security?
Tranquility?
That's cliche
At least I see you as a hero
But that's not a fair trade
I'm fucked up in the head
And this dread
It's eating me up alive

And you're just reading a book
You're doing something simple
So why am I putting all these barriers in front of me
Maybe I'll feel more confident if there was a riot
Happening around us
Because that's my world
And I can feel safe in that space
And yet
I'll still feel conflicted on what I will do
If you're getting burned
Push myself to get water-

Ah shit now you're leaving

I didn't even try to say hi
I couldn't do something that was so simple

But that's okay
You don't need me
And I don't deserve you
Especially with this fracture mind

And it will happen again
Nothing ever changes
Except for your being

But the dread remains the same

Men from the Same Womb

We came from the same womb
He was rebellious
This brother of mine
He was my role model
Always let me know what's right and what's wrong

He was a punk-man
Vegan-man
Hardcore-man
Metal-man
Straight Edge-man
Feminist-man
Bootboy-man
Communist-man
Atheist-man
And lady's gentleman-man

He was the man
I aspire to be
He took me under his wing
He was hard on me
To be his mini-me

Despite living under the same roof
We had different pasts
Six years apart
But the world changes so fast

I became the depressed-man
Anxious-man
Misanthrope-man
Confused-man
Denial-man
Lost-man
Theatrical-man
Poetic-man
Now medicated-man

Left me with the question
Who am I, man?

I always have the urge to call him
And tell him:
You piss me off, man
You failed me, man
You lied to me, man
You betrayed me, man
You left me behind, man
You should've been there every time
when I needed you, man
I wish I can kill your friends, man
So I can hurt you, man
But you don't deserve any of this shit, man

You've been through enough already
And I witnessed it
I know why you wanted to leave home so early

No matter how many times
You praise me
Compliment me
Encourage me
Uplift me
I'm still jealous of you, man
Because you have a past, man
You live in the present, man
You have a future, man
You are a teacher man
A counselor man
A husband man
Now a father man

And I'm still floating around like a balloon
So many times I thought I popped to stay grounded

None of this is your fault, man
So why the fuck am I angry at you, man?
How many times I wish I can call you
To tell you that your little brother is in crisis, man

Come home, man

But you got a life
And I shouldn't interfere

At the same time
I don't want to feel the need-to-need you
I can do this on my own
So you won't be my caregiver

But twenty years from now
I might be proven wrong

I'm stuck, man

Whenever I hear your voice on the phone
Asking me
"Hey man,
How have you been?"

And I always lie
By telling you
"Good man"

But I wish you knew, man
I wish I allowed you
To know, man

Machine Head

The son of a goddamn bitch
Also known as my father
Would come home from work every night
Had a habit of yelling at my dogs
Even when they're out of sight
They had to hear his grievances
My brother and I heard his
Through order and fear
"TURN OFF THE FUCKING LIGHTS!
TURN OFF THE FUCKING WATER!
OR WE ARE GOING TO GO BROKE AND STARVE
TO DEATH!"
And sometimes we felt it
By the belt

Somehow through his Sturm und Drang
We became prideful of our upbringing
Made us strong
We took hits
But kept going
We didn't complain
That's for pussies
People who don't work hard
This physical discipline was done to prepare us for our
Future employers

They will admire us for all the scars on our bodies
And psyche
Yet we manage to stay alive
To serve them with a smile and sheer determination
No matter our health
Not even our humanity
All to get that seventy-five cents raise
We are the working-class men
And we should feel proud of our endurance

...That's what we were groomed to believed

We wear Levi's 501 Jeans as a reminder of our
Past as working-class men
We glamorized communism for romanticizing the
Uprising of the working-class man
We humorized our pain to cope with our upbringing
As a working-class man
And we fantasize killing the rich to justify our crisis
For being the working-class man
My father was no longer seen as a villain
Just complicit to the grind that we dreamt
Destroying with a hammer and sickle

He is a machine head
Never said no to his employer
Always working at their order
On their time
Under financial chokehold

It's challenging to imagine him as a human being
Makes me wonder what his life would be like if he were
Flesh and metal is all I see in him
My Father
The body horror

He wants to go back home
Unfortunately he assimilated to this strange land
Now he feels a stranger at home
A lost boy
That left his mother to become the avatar of the Twelve-hour grind
He masquerades his pain and isolation by blasting
Tropical music
To remind him of home
Home where he tells us about stories such as a
Rattlesnake almost biting his brother's ass
While taking a shit
Home where he saw UFOs lighting up his house
Home where ghosts rearrange his aunts' dishes
Home where leprechauns lead people lost in the forest
Also,
Home where he was raised as a peon
Home where both his mother and father left him
Home where he was beaten as a reminder of who
He is and what he is meant to be

And he continued that tradition through me
Brainwashing me into thinking that people will value
Me more if I shut up and do what they say
And I'll get my just reward

A foolish pride that comes from a genetic lie
As he was given the pink slip
With no celebration
After 35 years
Just shitted out
Left to dry

Looking back his verbal and physical rage
I realized what he was saying all this time
"Welcome to the machine, my son"
His only hope to justify his existence is to have his
Last name carry on

But I won't make it happen

It ends with me

This is how you execute a working-class man
To leave him paralyzed
Like a legless insect
As his employer left him
Just as I'll leave his legacy

Now
He is waiting to be buried in the ground
But he knows in his heart
He already knows
He's buried alive

All The Quiet Underdogs on the Western Front

"I don't know man"
My brother will say to me
With uncertainty
About our place in this world

I question him
"After all we went through
All the beatings and surviving the hood,
Will it be worth it?"

Are we going to get our just reward?
We deserve it
We didn't fall from grace
We succeeded by overcoming the obstacles
We were born to lose

But we kept on striving
Proved everyone wrong
We didn't kneel to others expectations
We made our parents proud
Made everyone respect our parents when they know about
Our resilience

We left South Central that was supposed to devour
Our humanity

Even after all that
What is this reward we were supposed to receive?
Just a nice house, that's it?

Not asking for billions of dollars
Because I know what that will bring

Not even asking for a woman anymore
Because I'll be too much of a burden to them
Don't want to make them feel like home care nurses

Not even asking what it is to be a man anymore
Because it seems everyone wants to throw
Themselves in a rat race
Hoping to be buried like the kings of Egypt

I'm just asking for peace
But I doubt that's happening anytime soon
And I don't want to struggle anymore
But we are always going to end up struggling
If we runaway
Survivor's guilt will catch up to us
Reminding us of the people we abandoned

And all of our victories will feel hollow
Because we convinced ourselves that it was never
Truly ours
Despite of our frustration
Disillusionment
Resentment
Hopelessness
Rage
Depression
We will tell ourselves
"all is quiet on the western front"

But the noise will never leave us
Our neverending tinnitus

"Will it be worth it in the end?"

    "I don't know man,"
He says
Our eyes locked on the ground
Cold silence deafens my optimism

    "If anything
    Just do what makes you happy
    Be a good person
    Which is too much to ask for now
    Nobody can save us
    We have to save ourselves
    Just don't lose yourself
    You got me, man

You got our parents
Our sisters
Our nieces
Reach to me when you need to
That's all I can tell you"

After every philosophical discussion
He reassures me by saying:

"I love you"

We fade back into darkness

The Loaf of Bread from Sam's Club that Was Left Unsupervised on the Kitchen Table

You joked how my siblings and I
Get easily traumatized
Telling us we are soft like a sponge
Get easily soaked with emotions
Demanding my brother and me to not act
Like bitches and man up

You're the big man in the house
Power follows you
Until
A loaf of bread from Sam's Club was left
Unsupervised on the kitchen table
And you broke down
You lost control
You cursed at the skies
Demanding God why we didn't put the bread away
After we were done
You were far more dramatic than those TV parents
Finding out kids were doing drugs or getting
Pregnant
You deserve an Emmy

You stomped around

My mother trying to console you
But you locked yourself in the room
My siblings and I were left...traumatized

It was a Saturday afternoon,
Trying to make sense of your outburst
"What made him snap? He has never been in a war!"

But then I realized
That your outrage has led to your weakness
And I can use that for my advantage
I just have to focus
I began to recollect every moment how you felt
Claustrophobic
Around people in chaotic settings
Bringing up excuses on why you can't go to a fair

All the anxieties you hid through your brute nature
I once saw you as a no-nonsense blue collar
That disregards any form of entertainment
I now realize you're just a scared little boy
That wants to go back home to his mommy
But you've been so far away from home
That you lost your own footing

Sure you got respect
Sure they see you as an example of coming from
        Nothing to have Something

Sure you got a title and they bowed before you
But
I can take all of that away from you
I can tell you about my downfall
Where I was left unsupervised
That lasted only twenty minutes
A small-time frame of history
that could disappear in the world,
And no one would give a fuck about
Such a small number and small event that doesn't
Matter in the world at large
But it will matter to you
It will harm you
It will break you
It will undo you

That brings me to my final realization
I have the power now

And I have you in the palm of my hand
I can slowly crush you
When you saw me as a confused and frail being
I now become your horror
The door that should never be opened
Your end

And it's all thanks to the loaf of bread from Sam's Club
That was left unsupervised on the kitchen table

Facehugger

It straps on my face at nights
Not to impregnate me
And give birth to a
Darkly
Grotesque
And yet
Subjectively beautiful alien Xenomorph
But to feed me all the air
That I need
So I can sleep peacefully
Wake up with energy
And go on with my life

This CPAP machine
That makes me see myself as
Luke Skywalker in the streets
And Darth Vader in the bed sheets

Despite my self deprecating humor
I use as an excuse
To not bring anyone home
I use as an excuse
To not to stay at anyone's home

This mechanical umbilical cord
Reminds me why
I should always be on my own

I could destroy it
As my father always tried to convince me
"This medical condition
Is all in your head
The doctors just want your money
Spend that money on a hooker
And you will never have to use that shit again"

I went one night without it
Slept freely
In whatever position
That my body felt comfortable in

But woke up
With this dread
The depression came back
Forced me to walk with my head down
To hide from all the faces
Amplifying my anxieties
Beating to my head
As if to tell me
"It's good to be back in your head
I'm going to remind you
All the guilt
The shame
That you can't runaway

Remind you to see the world on fire
With this everlasting lustful desire
To feel and to commit ultra violence
And with this longing
To be dead"

This familiar voice
With it's dark cloud
That hovered over me
For most of my life
And this goddamn machine
It's the only thing
That provides the sunlight
That my mind needs

I only wish
There was a ghost in this machine
So it can speak to me
Keep me company
So I can stop tossing and turning at night

This cursed machine
It is the only thing
That keeps me
From falling into the abyss of insanity

The only thing
That I have to carry with me
Into my final sleep

A Different Type of Monster

"Vaaaalgame Diooooos."
In English it means "Oh my goodness."
Yeah, it's not stressing.
It does not emphasize the situation.
But my mother's saying of "Vaaaalgame Diooooos,"
tells you the story of
how everything was built
then slowly crumbled
into decay.
Think of Ozymandias,
men rose and then fell into oblivion.

My mother will always say "válgame dios"
whenever my dad screws up.
I wouldn't be surprised if my dad was the inspiration
for that phrase.
I use it on him too.
It pisses him off.
Storming away to lock himself in a room
and I laugh.

But I don't take into account how he feels.
He is a big man.
He can handle anything.
That's how I see him.

But what goes on in his head?
How can a simple man operate in a large
ever-changing world without losing his role?
Is this why he stays on the grind?
In his own comfort where his body suffers?
Has he ever wondered about being somewhere new?
Speaking up instead of talking down?

I've been told to try to understand him
and I do.

He's scared.

He doesn't admit it
His role prevents him,
And what will I see in him when he does?
Should I embrace him or should I pity him?
Can't tell this anger towards him
is either well-deserved or overdue.

Part of this endless frustration is karma;
his father was a sexual violator,
based on the hints that were given to us by his family.
And I am a sexual survivor.
Although,
he doesn't know that about me yet.
To keep that away from him is an act of mercy.

And what will that do to a simple man?
In knowing he's right in between two extremes?

While I never met his father,
We do have something in common:
we abandoned him.
Don't want anything to do with him,
just ignore him.
For his father gave him life,
perhaps through force,
I could end it
through words.
A different type of monster I'll become.

Look on my works, ye Mighty, and despair.

If I do this
I know what my mother will say to me,
who she raised to be a good person with a kind heart:
"Vaaaaalgame diooooos."

Destiny

I'm the bastard of South Central
I left you all behind
I was told to
I was demanded to
I was ordered to do

I am the bastard child of district #9
It has forgotten me
To appease those that are higher than me
Left me in jealousy
It ruined me

I am my community's runaway
I didn't believe in all of you
We are dreamers
But never rulers

I am my home's traitor
This is how I define myself when I'm drunk
I'm looking out for myself but not the rest
I am not a savior
I am an escaper

I am in damnation
Linger to what could have been

If I was brave
But my mouth was covered
As I always run for cover

I am a coward
I am not for defiance as I wish to be
I curse myself everyday
To my dying day
That's my destiny

Poor Boy

Poor boy you're alone
Poor boy you're dancing by yourself
Poor boy you're too shy to ask for her name
Poor boy you think she'll be is disgusted by you
Poor boy you know you cannot make her cum
Poor boy you're too null
Poor boy you think you're healing but you're not
Poor boy you're walking away from the club
with your head down
Poor boy you'll soon become a poor old man
Poor boy you're on the bus getting home
Poor boy you're sleeping on your own
Poor boy you're dreading with your cpap machine
Poor boy you keep repeating the same thing over again

Nothing changes

Let me change you
Let me shame you
Let me dehumanize you
Let me choke you
Let me destroy you

Poor boy

Let me in

Winback

Give me back my violence
Let me inflict pain
Let me fight back
Let my hands spilt blood from their faces
Let me have my dominance
Let me have my breakdown
Let me wield a broken shard glass
And stab my own hand with it
Let my blood stream down to the Earth
Let it become an earthquake
To let everyone know I have come back
Let their dismissal faces become
The true definition of horror

Let me become my own horror
I don't care If I become their monster
I needed to become my own savior
Let me have my voice become terror
To make them heed me
Even when I'm not around

Let me traumatize them

Let me become fear

I implore you God
Let me have my violence back
Because without it
I am a clown

Candy

I told myself the biggest lie
I said
"I don't need anybody,
I'm fine on my own
I know how to get by"

I told myself that lie
With extreme confidence
And underlying sadness
Knowing my hands
Will be the only thing
That will cover me with blankets
To keep me warm at night

I keep telling myself that lie
So I don't feel guilty of not even
Trying to hold someone else's hand
And ask
"What do you think of that movie?
Can I get playfully jealous with you if you tell me
That actor was fine?"

Oh how I love telling myself that lie
So I can go to restaurants on my own
Without waiting for hours in line

Walking by those annoying couples
Smiling
Telling each other stories
Breathing each other's life
But at least
I had my tummy filled
So that's fine

Oh, how I used my trauma
To excuse that lie
Telling myself
"I need to heal myself completely first
Before I can let someone in
To kiss me goodnight"

I love that lie
Because it comforts me
And it is easy to believe

But that lie is killing me
I know this
But I still eat it
Like candy

Drunk Poem

Cousin telling me about his trip to Argentina
Forgot witch city but not Buenas Aires
Mountains with snow
Summer is winter
Another cousin talked about the unbroken chain
Father always suffers for his son
Unheard of, unpopular
Enjoy time with parents, he says
I need to enjoys time with dad
When mom passes away I'll be fine
When dad passes away I won't be okay
Make peace with him
He's not a bad man
He's doing the best he can
Despite all the obstacles given to him
Clearly, I wrote something clearly while drunk

I need to get that cake
Kid it's in my way
I wish I could kick her and send her to the moon so
I can get that cake
I'm going to dance with the cake
And give ok sign to dad when dancing
I am hoping this woman I'm dancing with right now
Is not my cousin

She's fucking hot
Jerk off memory is stored
But I need that fucking cake
Fuck...out...my way I need to devour the cake
Make peace with dad in the end
And stuff my face with cake
Cake is good
Tres leches is ducking good
Fuck you iPhone corrected me

VI. Mime Speaks

Your Silent Face

I picked your face to be mine
Your face
Is quietly expressive
Through colorful emotions

I picked your face
Because I feel safe
And I feel free

Anyone who wears your face
Hides their pain
For the sake of others' enjoyment

However
Your face and others like yours
Became twistedly manufactured to be feared
To sell movies and masks
There were some that used it to hide
their sadistic intentions

But that's not your face

When I sketch you on my face
We become silly
We become embarrassing

We become sassy
We become beautiful

We can be outgoing
Pretending to dance with someone
Leaving the audience amused

But when I wipe you off
I go back to being the observer
And lonely

I like your face
It's a reflection of my desire to be alive
It can also be seen as a mirror
How society has become a circus
And I can safely dance in chaos

It feels therapeutic
When I draw you on my face
So many colors to choose from
For a colorless face

So many variations
Whiteface, Tramp, Rodeo, Creepy, Jester
But you, Mime,
I choose your silent face
Even though you're in black and white
You still have a greater depth

You were taught not to speak
And I was taught not to speak up for myself
For fear of receiving a harsher punishment

But we will change that
No longer should we compromise
We will speak up
And when we do
People will listen
We will see their faces change
Into various expressions
Perhaps
We can help them unravel their true faces

Our silent face
Is our shield
Our power
And our salvation

Accent

My accent materialized on 84th Place
Between Wall and Main
It moves with the urgency of trying to get home
Before the Sun comes down
It moves like a paranoid criminal
Thinking it's going to get killed any minute
Any second
As a bystander

Sometimes it feels relaxed knowing it accepted
Death at a young age
Sometimes it doesn't want to move at all
Wanting the A-bomb to drop so it doesn't have to
Live in fear anymore

Sometimes it feels frustrated
Trying to get words to sound superficially clear
Because clarity was horror
Clarity was powerless
Clarity was submission
Clarity was all the fucked-up shit
That was absorbed from this street

It was born with a mother's tongue
But it was ordered to speak with
The "powers that be" tongue
Because that's how you can make it out alive
Have success
Living in a white picket fence
With a dog named Rex

My tongue used to move by evading fear that came
Home every night at 9
The tired man wanted everyone to be quiet
Living paycheck to paycheck developed a harsh noise
That the tongue didn't know how to respond to
But it gave up knowing any response
Will lead to harsh discipline

The tonality of the tongue was shaped by picking
Up patterns on how life was breathed
And was taken away
It was in awe of the '92 riots
It moved with confusion of seeing bloods and crips
Getting along
Chaotic peace
It tried to fuse with the slang from the Black and
Brown ruling the streets
But the conflict of those two left the tongue in idle

The tongue picked up static
From distorted violence running the streets
All that makes the tongue want to break free
From conflicted structures and lay rest on the beach
It wants to move with the calm waves of the ocean

But the damage has already been done
There's no going back to relearn the standard patterns
The emotions of this human soul are in a constant struggle
Even though the streets are no longer speaking in blood
It still speaks from the past
Reminding the tongue
To let everyone know it survived a harsher past
And to move with pride and defiance when it gets asked
"Where is your accent from?"
And to say it with self-respect
For they better recognize
As I will regulate by saying
"My accent is a South Central accent.
Biatch!"

Identity Crisis

Mexican
Mexican-American
Hispanic
Chicano
American
Latino
Latinx
Each with a bubble
I don't know which one to fill in
Each label with its own archetype
But none of it applies to me
I leave it empty

I don't know who I am
What I am
What I'm destined to be

I got no home
Here in the states,
Where I was born
People think I'm from my parents' birth home
When I go to my parents' birth home
They know I'm from the place where I was born
They called me Ghost
I just hovered around aimlessly

I got no country,
No land to say you belong here without question
I am an outsider
With no place to call home
Just a room that I'm familiar with
That I shielded myself from animosity and conformity
My only best friend is the imagination of a better
World
Where I belong

And yet I don't want to belong to myself
Because my true self wishes the destruction of the world
The pain, the hate, the fear, the resentment,
I thought I would grow out of it
But I'm wrong
I don't know how to let it go
And I don't want it to be by sucking the breast of a woman
Once she's gone
I'll go back to sucking my thumb
Everyone will know
That I haven't grown

"Love yourself" they say
"Be yourself," they say
How can you do that?
When the very people who said that
Will gently push you away
They can't comprehend your fully exposed being
Weird is a word they like to own, and yet,
They don't fully know

Who am I?
Where should I go?
What do I need to do to feel validated?
When is it supposed to start?
Where do I belong?
Whom do I belong to?
Who I'm destined to be?
Who should hold the answers?
All this life that I'm surrounded by,
Is nothing but a mirage
As I am still stranded in the desert
Asking for answers

Tough Love

Fuck the Dodgers
Fuck the Lakers
Fuck the Raiders
And fuck the Rams

Fuck your souped up Honda
Fuck you dream Maserati
Fuck you mom's Silverado truck
And fuck your dad's Tacoma truck

Fuck your LA hats
Fuck your LA tattoos
Fuck your jerseys
And fuck your Jordans too

Fuck your love for Kobe
Fuck your love for NWA
Because fuck your love for the police

Fuck your cousin and his LAPD crew
Fuck your uncle and his Sherriff department clique
Fuck your friend with his fade-ass haircut and
Real Estate business
And fuck all their wives for not clapping back at
Their abusive moms

Fuck your dad's job
Fuck his pride in his underpaid twelve hour ethic
Fuck your dad's justification of his abuse
And fuck you for convincing yourself it made you tough
Because you know your ass has already been
Triggered by what I've said so far

Fuck your disdain towards immigrants
And fuck your parents for bending their asses for
Their white masters
Fuck your victim blaming
On top of that
Fuck your mom,
Who you learn that shit from
And fuck your abuela
For blaming your Tia for being raped

Fuck your Mexican flags
A land that will never claim you
Fuck your US flags
A land that will get rid of you
if you don't submit to their game

Fuck Vicente Fernandez
And fuck Morrissey
Those rich fucks are not from LA
So why should we give a fuck about them?

Fuck your lack of love for your community
Fuck your "what about this or that?" ideology
Fuck your "it is what it is"
And fuck your submission to the status quo

However,
Fuck me for giving up on you
Fuck me for not having faith in you
Fuck me for disowning you
And fuck me for wanting to be on my own

From beretta hats to LA Dodger hats
From raised fist to holding benjamins
From Pancho Villa to Donald J Trump
From no stinking badges to work ID badges

Fuck us for selling out

With tough love

Sincerely yours,

South Central

Latino/Hispanic Pyramid Scheme

Latinx
A word that is often accused by prideful Hispanics and/or Latinos
as being a white's man term
And yet
These prideful people
Speak and think in white men's language
And are sports franchise fanatics
That are owned by white men
Work for their white bosses
And marry white people
Even the label Hispanic and Latino
Were created by white men
Latinx is a word that is accused of being a tool
Used by white people to separate us

Bullshit

We separate ourselves

We built a pyramid
Both Mexican Americans and Cuban Americans
Seeing themselves at the top
While Salvadorans
Guatemalan
Hondurans

Puerto Ricans
Dominicans
And others that struggle the same as we do
Are seen as the bottom
We treat them as such
This is not the white men's doing
It is our parents doing

White men are just amused by it
Impressed even
But we were raised to impress them
Raised to bend our backs for them
But we won't do it for ourselves

We don't got each other's back
We don't protest against the unjust that has been done to us
"That's happening to them, not me"
"That happened a long time ago! We are not Black foo! Forget about that shit!"

Vanessa Guillen's death was covered by the military
We still went to work
Opening day Dodger game
We call in sick
And we still complain about how nobody cares about us

We criticize Black people for acting like the victims
And yet
It was a Black person that taught me about the lynching of
Mexicans and Mexican Americans in the early 1900s
And we still antagonized them
That's a white men's mentality

Latinx did not separate us
It reminded us how we are ourselves
And how we decide what makes a Latino
Disregard those that don't fit into traditional lifestyle
The irony of these prideful Hispanics and/or Latinos
Is that they wave their Mexican and Cuban flags
And visualize claiming the land as theirs
With open arms
And they will be seen as kings and queens
That will liberate the people
Hoping they will be treated as such
Again that's a white men's mentali–No...

That's a...colonizer's mentality

'Member Pancho Villa?
Do you think that he would have sided with
Che Guevara
or with LA's Sheriff's Department?

Mexico and Cuba
The countries that our parents ran away from

But still we believe we will go there to claim it
And make it better

But the countries and their people won't claim us
Forever seeing us as outsiders
Half-breed bastards
That will be disgusted taking a shit on a toilet with no seat
That will complain about the tropical heat
That will worry about not getting wifi
Not able to buy jerseys and luxurious clothing

Thinking two weeks vacation is all we need
To feel like our people
But the triangle gets broken
Our sense of importance will be laughable
The countries people will tell us:
"You don't know the paths of this living as you wish you did. You
can survive it but you won't learn from it. You can buy our land,
but our culture is not for sale...not even for you. Go back home to
your Disneyland and Netflix"

We will go back home
Feeling betrayed
But we will hope for the white men to do the job for us

And when the job is done
We comfort ourselves by saying
"That happened to them, not us. That happened a long time
ago! We are not black foo! You're acting like white liberal. Stop
complaining about that shit!"

She Walked On Her Own That Night

She walked on her own that night
As she got off
On a lonely bus stop
Only a faint street light
That does not provide a ray of hope

She walked on that dark path
That will swallow any brave soul

My cousin
Who became numb
By seeing corpses left behind by the cartels
Even said
"That's a dark path that I will never walk on my own"

She walked on her own that night
Where is she coming from?
Where is she going?
Why isn't anybody with her?
Why isn't anybody waiting for her?

She walked on her own that night
And I cannot stop thinking about it
All I can do is write about it
Because she is a woman

If she was a guy
It would've been boring
Uninspiring
Depressing
Dull
I know this
Because I walk on my own at night

Every lonely night

With the longing for companionship
With the longing for feeling anew
And other hopeless romantic shit you can think of

But this isn't about me
This is about her
I want and need you to know that
This woman walked on her own that night
Because I am afraid for her

All the stories I've heard
Throughout my whole life
That always starts with:
She was walking to school
She was coming back from work
She was going to the store to buy milk
She just wanted to walk during daylight

Daylight

All those stories
Reassured me that
That she won't make it home that night

She won't make it home to her mom
She won't make it home to her dad
She won't make it home to her sisters and brothers
She won't make it home to her child
She won't make it home to her love

She won't make it home that night

And I did nothing about it
I allowed it
We allowed it
And we will blame her for it
And joke about it
That's all we can do

Maybe
Just maybe
She walked on her own that night
Because she knew how to walk on her own at night
She knew the darkness
She danced in it
She used it to hide herself from the evil light

She walked on her own that night
Because she might have been a vengeful spirit

A foolish hope
That I hope is true

She walked on her own that night
And I admired her
For defying my fear
For defying the social contract

And I was jealous of her bravery
She walked on her own that night
So many things
Ran through my mind
But in the end
I hope she made it home that night
The same way I always make it home

Unbothered
Unfollowed
Untouched
Unscathed

Just Safe

Narcoleptic

Let me sleep on this couch
I know I ate too much
And it can mess me up
My mom will tell you that I can die
Maybe she's wrong
Or maybe she's right
But still

Let me sleep right now
I'm surrounded with joy
Which puts my mind and body at ease
Better than tossing and turning in the dark
I know it's afternoon
And my mom will tell you that I sleep at random times
And at random places
Be it ceremonies, parties, nightclubs and my
Sister's in-law's house
They have a nice couch

You'll laugh when my brother tells you
That I slept on my very first date
In her car
While she was talking
You will end up saying
"Poor girl, man, poor girl"

And my sister will shake her head with embarrassment
For she's the one who set up the date
"That little punk, I should've punch him when he got home"
she'll say

Let me sleep, dude
Because I think I'm narcoleptic
Maybe it's a food coma
Since I just finished the plate of carne asada,
con arroz blanco,
y frijoles negros,
cebollitas,
guacamole,
salsa roja,
tortillas de Amapola,
Drinking that ice cold can of Coca-Cola
Followed by platanos asado con café de Folgers
Lastly,
Hearing both my mom's and dad's laughter
All those simple things
That's doesn't matter to the world at large
But it matters to me
And I take it with me

Let me sleep, foo!
I'm allowing myself to rest
I didn't drink sleeping teas
Nyquil, tequila, vodka or whiskey
And don't remind me to use that CPAP machine
I just want my body to rest naturally

Let me sleep, man
Because I've been through enough already
And I'm tired of pretending that I haven't
I know I'm not old
But I grew up fast
Tell me to pull myself up by my bootstraps
And I'll promise you
I'll will wear and tear them by the beginning of Spring
Besides
I'm listening to my body
Not you

Let me sleep
I'm in my momma's house
It's warm
And I got nothing to worry about
Is a place for me to dream
If you can
Please be kind
By throwing me a blanket
Preferably San Marcos blanket from Tijuana
Make sure it's the green one with the
German Shepherd family
It's 30 years-old but still works

Just let me sleep on this couch
If I don't wake up
That's alright
Just do me a favor
And I never ask for favors
But just this one
Coming straight from the heart
Remind my mom
That I left the world
The way that I wanted to leave
With a belly filled with love
And with joyful laughter
From those who I love
In this lively, peaceful scenery
That will serve as the closing act
In my own Long Days Journey Into the Night

Hot Mess

I am hot
And I have trauma
Which makes me a hot mess

I order chocolate martinis in sports bars
Because I am a hot mess
I have exquisite taste in movies and music
Because I am a hot mess
And I want to bite a corgi's butt
Because I am a hot mess

I like to lay down on my queen size plush pillow-top bed
Cover myself in Liz Clairborne liquid cotton 400
Thread count bed sheets from JC Penney
And masturbate to hentai
Because I am a hot mess

Oh I'm sorry
Did I disgust you?!
Were you expecting me to be a Don Juan?
Where I slept with all the girls I've met at bars or clubs?
That's my fantasy too you know
But I have it a hard time making it a reality
Due to my abusive childhood past
That really brought down my self-esteem

Amplifying my insecurities
To the extent that I cannot perform in bed
Leaving me seeking solace in my own fantasies
Where I feel free from the sexual trauma
That has been inflicted upon me
Leaving me with the everlasting desire to
Experience sexual healing
Where the little boy in me won't feel any harm
I am sorry, mija,
I am not who you thought I was
But I am trying to be
Who I need me to be
Because I am a hot mess

I am yearning for the day where
I will be gently touched
But I am very picky
Because I am hot a mess

Fear not
I am taking therapy
And writing poetry
Because I am a hot mess

And thanks to Barbie
I am Kenough to say that I am a
Hot mess

VII. Reclaim

Stay

I was supposed to die in Transylvania
For being an idiot
I took a shot of one Jagermeister
Three shots of Brandy
Two glasses of red wine
And five bottles of beer
All under two hours

The last thing I remember
I was dancing with a trio of mimes
In one of Dracula's castles
On Halloween night

I could've had a poetic death
A virgin dying in the land of the Prince of Darkness

I didn't even suffer
It was the best way to go
I didn't think of all the mistakes I've done
Or things I would've done differently
I was having fun
With no care
It would've been the best way to go

But my peaceful death was stopped
By a little girl
Who saw me on my back
Vomiting
She called the ambulance

She wasn't supposed to be there
It was an adult party
But the Make -A-Wish Foundation made it so
It was her wish to party in one of Dracula's Castles
And her older brother hooked me up with the drinks

And she was in remission

That little teenager was beating Death
To save my dumbass from Death
In her case
She was defiant
In my case
I was a fool

I knew I was going over my limit
I should have stopped
But I didn't
Because I wasn't afraid anymore
I was feeling free
The best way to greet Death
And the wrong way to say goodbye

The first words I heard in my rebirth was
"Stay"
Coming from the nurse's mouth
As I was being delirious
Confused
Frightened
He suppressed my will to leave the hospital bed
"No, Stay"
He said again
And I listened

When I heard it was a girl that saved my life
I was happy
I became hopeful
I told myself "It was meant to be! My romantic life is going to start"
She is my Elisabeta!"
Then I was told she was part of the
Make-A-Wish Foundation
I thought to myself "Maaan, she has a tough job!
I'm going to promise myself
Not to make her go through that shit again"
Then I was corrected when they told me
"She's a cancer survivor and she is sixteen!"
Ah fuck me
I was saved so I can suffer more?

But I thanked her
By letting her keep my costume hat
As a reminder of the dumbass who she saved
She prevented my parent's wedding anniversary
from becoming a memorial of my demise

Imagine that
Married on Halloween
And their child's lifeless body is far away
Far away from their senses

And I owe it to her
I owe it to myself
And I owe it to us survivors

And here I am

I'm here to stay.

Thirty-Seven

Thirty-seven years
Is how long it took me to see you as a person
A father
A lifeform not motivated by fear
Not fused with machinery
Not shaped by the economy

Your true form
Laid back
Dreaming buying
The land
Home where you grew up with your mother and
Siblings
They're all gone now
But you still want it to honor them
To see their ghosts
Talk to them when no one is around

A house built for your children and grandchildren to
Visit
Tell us stories
That goes well with the environment

Growing a farm
For you to harvest

Have your hands and feet on the soil
Not metal
Just pure Earth
On which you were raised in
Where you hope to be buried
Thirty-seven years
Is how long it took me to realize it
Since I was blinded by your rage
That was fueled by your separation anxiety
Of being away from home

Thirty-seven years
Is how long it took me to be alone with you
For more than a half an hour
Without feeling any resentment towards you
Without feeling the urge to ignore you
Without giving you one-word answers
Without feeling forced to give you a complete
Sentence

Now we are in your home
And it took thirty-seven years
To treasured each other's company

We had conversations
We communicated

For the past thirty-seven years
You would ask me the name of the deceased
Singer from AC/DC

You keep asking that same question
You know it already
It is Bon Scott
What I didn't know
Is that you were trying to reach me

Thirty-seven years
Is how long it took you to genuinely smile at me
Not by bringing a woman over to the house
But by busting my moves on the dance floor
In your homeland
As your family and friends were cheering me on
As I was feeling free
Dancing is my therapy
And you were proud of me

This vacation
Where we were both free from digital clocks
Free from getting pissed off at rising prices
Free from being stuck at homes
Free from survival mode
Free from feeling like strangers in the "land of the free"

Unfortunately

You couldn't share a drink with me
Alcohol poisoning and violence is what made you stop
Hasn't touched a bottle for 33 years
Didn't want to risk going back to being
A Machine Head again

As much as you want to forfeit
For just one shot
That'll last no longer than a second
With your son as a bonding moment
You couldn't break that promise you made for us
And for yourself
A sacrifice that you will carry to your well-deserved
Peaceful end

Now that I am in your habitat
I fully realize how your form came to be
You are with your people
I could see glimpses of your childhood
Who you were
What kind of trouble you got yourself into
Makes me imagine your youthful laughter
Your youthful cries
And your youthful dreams
Makes me wonder how fast you ran
Makes me wonder what you saw in this world
Makes me wonder what you dreamt
You were child of this Earth
That was molded into this wicked industrial
Machinery
For survival
A horrendous transition

From aria to dissonance

All I had gotten before were snippets of your
Childhood
That was distorted by the sound of fury
To my life's composition

Now
As part of you true atmosphere
I get it
I understand your rhythm
What patterns you dance
The melodies you react to joyfully

As much as you want it
As much as you wish
You accept that I cannot compose a song
That equally matches your wavelength
But you fully appreciate that I allow myself
To meet you halfway
And to improvise with you to the end
Without judgment
Without resentment

Just pure love

Mr. Nintendo

A little gray box lays in my room
He calls himself Nintendo
He was my parents' co-parent
Yet my dad hated him
I spent so much time with him

But he doesn't know Nintendo like I do
When the streets were on fire
Nintendo would tell me
"Stay inside
I'll keep you safe
You're scared
I'll help you become brave
Press the power button
I'll take you to a different world"

I pressed the button and his heart glowed red
He gave me his control
Tells me
"You are in control
Whatever happens
It's up to you."

Nintendo made me feel invincible when I touched a Star
Made me feel powerful when I punched-out Mike Tyson

Made me feel like a hero when I rescued
A Princess and her Hyrule Kingdom
I was who I wanted to be that I couldn't be in the streets

But he wasn't always kind
He challenged me all the time
He was my electronic sensei
He beat me down with Contra
I got back up with Castlevania
Whenever I made a mistake
He told me to press reset,
Correct the mistake

Nintendo trained me to become a perfectionist
It knew there weren't extra lives in the real world

The Koopa Troopas of the neighborhood took my Controller away
Toyed with me to play with their own...Genesis Controller
Took advantage of me
That will give them five stars on Grand Theft Auto

The power adapter broke
The screen flashed green
Nintendo and I became useless
We became mechanical voids

Nintendo was locked away in the garage
Along with my mind,
My will

Collecting dust
For 30 years

Rather than burning the garage down
I decided to give us an extra life
I took us out of that dungeon
I gave ourselves a new power adapter
And I got my controller back

Finally
I beat Contra
Without using the Konami code

I now have the Power Glove

Triforce of Sisterhood

"You asshole" my sister signature phrase
She would call me that all the time
Jokingly of course
I told her "You're going to have a baby?
You are a feminist sellout!"

She strikes back with a 3-hit combo
"Oh whatever punk!
Loser!
You're mommy's favorite!"
The oldest of the 3 women I grew
Up with, the one I feel closest to

Yet,
I get easily annoyed asking
Me too many detailed questions
On things that are not important
She will cut me off with
"Wait-wait-wait-what kind of blue was it?
Sky blue or dark blue? Baby blue?"
I grudgingly answer
"-it doesn't matter,
It's not important part of the story"

"Oh yeah, that's right
Sorry about that brother, keep going
OH MY GOD LOOK AT THAT CAR
Doesn't that car remind you of our old car?"
Hyper aware is how I would describe her

I always reach out to her whenever
I get anxiety attacks
Needing to hear her voice
Reassuring me of our place in the U.S.
A country threatening her freedom
Her existence, for being a woman
I always check on her
Expecting her to vent
But she remains calm, collective and in control
While I express my worries and frustrations
Of not doing enough for her
She guides my emotions, centering me
Consoling me
"Yes brother, it's bad, it's scary
Thankfully young people
Are becoming more aware
They're more active
There's hope
No, you are not going to assassinate a politician
I would feel honored
But you have to think about our mom
She is sick, you gotta be there for her
Carne asada is this Sunday
We need you to get on dad's nerves

for being a freeloader, please
bring a lot of Tupperware"
She is far more optimistic than I am
How I wish I had her wisdom

"Oh really"
My second sister's signature phrase
She doesn't let me get away
With my bullshit
"Yep"
She will monotonically respond
Whenever I admit my mistakes
She's always on to me
She'll always give me that suspicious stare
She instinctively knows I'm hiding something
Especially when I told our mom that
I had one drink
She always knows I had more than three
She lets out:
"Hmmmmm...."

Our tough upbringing made me
Hate her,
Our father shut me down for her
I am no physical match
I bullied her
To get back at him
Criticized her every decision
Never logically sound

We are at peace now
I still feel resentment towards myself
She forgives me

"Well yeah, you were a jerk
But I was a jerk too
That was a long time ago
Seriously, it's cool
It's okay
Just let that go"

I can't

She deals with grief
Personal loss
Expected her to unleash
all her fury towards me
She didn't
We hug
Keeps her head up
Moves on
She's stronger than me
How I wish I had her power to overcome and forgive

"Oh hey"
Simple signature phrase belonging
to my baby sister
She looks up to me
That scares me
I don't want to be a role
Model for anybody
I'm not mentally sound

We talk, share our taste for movies and tv shows
She's goal oriented
Always trying something new
Seeking my opinion on things
She shows interest
What does she see in me that I don't?
I am just overthinking everything
She is younger than me
She has so much more
Life experiences

She lived in Russia during the war
I lived in isolation in my LA apartment
She calls me
"Yeah I like it here
Everybody here has their own style
And I don't get stressed out seeing a doctor
I'm more relax here

But I do miss you guys
So, how have you been?
What have you been up to?"
It feels like a challenge
I lie
Don't want her to know the truth
Don't want to be fragile
Have to be strong
She's far braver than me
She still looks up to me

How I wish I had her courage

Three sisters who I envy
Their Wisdom
Their Power
And Their Courage

I imagine a world where they have their own
Queendoms

I don't want to imagine a world without them
Even after this world
I forever want to be reincarnated as their brother
I forever want to be Link
To these three Goddesses

"The Triforce of Sisterhood"

Your Little Bitch Is Now Your Pimp

I gave you a spotlight
I gave you a voice
But what you didn't know
Is that you're under my control

I put you on stage
For 4 minutes and that's it
But once you're done
I get my pay

After all is said and done
They will only know me by my name
Then you will know
That your "little bitch"
Is now your pimp

The Storm (little Boy pt.3)

I storm the dungeon of my mental depression
To find and end the Little Boy
Kill him with extreme prejudice

I descended the stairs of my insanity
Found myself in a long hallway consisting of
Twenty-four cells
Each cell consisted of a horrible version of me
That I fear to be

In one cell children were in a state of confusion,
And this me tells me through the looking glass:
"I'm just repeating the cycle
Our Little Boy doesn't mind
Besides
He's too weak to speak for himself
But look at the brightside
I'm creating artists like yourself
Now, go away you clown
You disgust me"

In the next cell
Saw me deprecating female bodies
And he tells me:
"What? Are you going to ask me why I don't think about

Our mother, sisters or nieces?
You are a funny guy
I don't love them
Our Little Boy doesn't care
He can't protect them
And so, I slaughter them
Respectfully of course
But you love them
Whatever strength they give you
Ain't nothing to compare to mine
Now leave you're making me weak"

In the next cell
I saw me mutilating myself
Swallowing razor blades,
Showering in battery acid
He tells me:
"Better me than them. I'm hurting me, and not them.
I'm a good person, right?"

Next cell was just a feather floating around
With no gap for it to escape

In the last cell
Saw an older version of me
Surrounded by nothingness
He tells me:
"I'm not like all these monsters here
I did good
But I give in to fear

I didn't even try to live
Always making up excuses
People have forgotten about me
This solitary is my punishment for pushing them away
Our Little Boy
God I wish I could've talked to him
But I ignored him
Which is why I am here"

All these cells connect to one room
The Control Room

A huge dark dome
Built and run by living machinery
Speaking to me in agonizing mechanical sounds
Questioning my presence with a low roar
And I answered it

"Show me the little boy
Or I'll go back out there and end myself
To leave you to rust"
A spotlight hit the center

And there he was

That small frail body
Beaten bruised
His sternum exposed
Each bone on his rib hooked by chains
With nerves

They are attached to the wall
Acting as a power source for the cells
His groin is festered with maggots
He is legless
But his phantom legs make him think he can walk
Stupid boy
His lower jaw dangling
Hanging on by a string
A centipede-like insect slowly devours his left arm
The boy screams in pain

But I remain silent
Something that he makes me do
When I'm out there in the world

He tries to crawl away
But his tail bone is hooked to the ground
He's trying to scream for his mommy
But he can't
So he begins to bang his head out of frustration
The hook on his tailbone slowly begins to twist
The boy cries in agony
The hook stops
The machines screech a sound like laughter

Disgusted by what I saw
I began to advance towards the Little Boy
Each footstep

His body pulses in fear
He tried to cower back
But there was no place to hide

I stand before him now
"You" I start
"You little bitch
All because of you
You held me back
For thirty-years
You made me feel beaten down
You took my will to sleep in peace
You took my will to love and be loved
You isolated me"

His tears begin to fall from his blind-ectropion eyes

"No matter how damaged you present yourself
You won't get any sympathy from me
This is where I detach myself from you
This is where you die"
Just as I was about to strike him down with my scythe
With all his might
He says
"I am s-s-sorryyyy"
"P-p-please loooove me"
He extends his arms to me
Like a child would do to their parent after a fall

I am my mother's child
I picked him up

He embraced me tightly
Quivering in fear
"I-I-I don't want to be h-h-here anymore
I want to g-g-go hooome"

The exact same words that I tell myself when
I am somewhere where I don't want to be
I could feel his decaying heart beating close to mine
At the same pace
"I will" I told him as I close my arms around him

This place
This dark dome
It felt like it was built by memories that want to forget
"The bad memories Little Boy,
All the horrible memories chained you here
And it made me afraid when I am out there
But not all of then were bad
Remember our first memory
Our feet were up in the air
Our mom was changing our diaper
She was calling our dad
And then we call our dad by his first name
Do you remember her face?"
"Sh-sh-she was smiiiiling"
"Yes,
Now remember when we finally left home

To live on our own
The hug that she gave us
Before we drove away from her arms
Remember her embrace
And our tears
Just take it in,
Take the good in
Take in her light
And let it out"

The Little Boy let out a powerful scream
Filled with warmth and joy
A scream burning with the realization of the love he had
Slowly our bodies began to disintegrate
Our ashes took form into a whirlwind of fire
That melted the machinery that imprisoned him
We became a firestorm
That burned his dungeon
Along with the grotesque versions of ourselves
That fear
Burned down

We are storm
A force that is neither right nor wrong
And we can survive through it all
And we will move forward
To burn down our depression

The Perfect S'more

I want to be beautiful
I want to leave you in awe

I want to be as divine as all the cosmos in the sky
That will make you wonder and inspire you
To ascend beyond the galaxies
I want to be as scenic as the forest resting by the
Snowy mountains
With a lake that reflects the sky
And I want to be as dazzling as the morning sun
That gives you the energy to drive
Where you want and need to be

I want you to see me elevating
With flower petals gravitating around me
See me floating by a waterfall
See me morphing into a celestial being

My heart and soul are yearning to be as enchanting
As the soundtrack from the war film "The Thin Red Line"
They want to be as heavenly as the protagonist in the film
How he ran away from war
But was dragged back
Still kept that spark
That optimism of a better world

But was surrounded by Death
And accepted it
Without fear
Just calm

I want to be as beautiful as my mother's love
I want to be as beautiful as my father's joyful moments
And I want to be as beautiful as the embrace from my brother,
sisters and nieces

Lastly, I want to be as beautiful as the perfect s'more
In the microwave
How something so simple can make me forget all the woes
Puts me in a state of trance
Just enjoying my humanity
Being thankful to be alive to taste this beautiful creation

As much as I think that my current beauty
Falls under either dark or gothic beauty
Because of its intensity
Its visceral rawness
I know for a fact that it is an unrefined beauty

Like the sun that lights up the sky after a storm
Where you see the outlines of clouds
And their different shades of white and grey
Illuminated by different colors
The sun lights up my desolate environment
It is still vibrant with life

Because the darker the depth that the soul falls into
The brighter the light it ignites

My only wish
Is for this beauty to be ever constant
May its light never go out
To make me feel
Divine
Enchanting
Heavenly
And beautiful

Don't let the pancakes get cold

Swimming in the dark sea
Fighting against the raging tidal waves
Under violent storms
So many times I could've drown
But I kept on going

I became weightless
Let the waters move me
Because I lost myself

The sirens of the deep
Called my name
Sang melodies
Songs that I know by heart
Urging me to let go
To seek solace in that cold dark womb

Against my wishes
Against my desires
Against my comfort
I ignored their call

I lay on the ocean
Saw the stars that I'll never reach
Closed my eyes and let the icy water burn me
But then I felt a warm wave
Opened my eyes and saw the bluest sky
A hand pulled me to shore
A future me with a radiant glow

And he said to me,
"Hey man, that some crazyass shit you went through.
Come on, the pancakes are getting cold."

Barbed Wires

You lost something
Actually, you lost yourself
You keep running to reach that field
That promises you peace
So you can lie down
And disappear with serenity

I know that feeling
Because I am that feeling
The desire to feel whole
The desire to feel ease
And the everlasting desire to be happy

You are afloat
With the dire need to be grounded
So you can feel every step you take
To get to that field

And I being your frustration
Your anger
Your sadness
And your tears

But I am not your trauma
I am a symptom of it
And I wish I wasn't

You can either dilute or enrich me with alcohol
You want to blackout
But I'll keep you up
So you won't give up
On speaking up

And we express it beautifully
And darkly
Through words
On the stage
Or by dancing to songs
Hoping our mental scars will fade away

But please
Don't think of me as your specter
For I feel your pain too

I don't want to be your longing anymore
I am tired
Just as you are

You need to bid farewell to your past
Cut those barbed wires that's been holding you
Back
So you can reach to the end of that path
And once you do

You will lie down on that grassy field
Right under the sun
You will feel all the colors
To reclaim your human right
And I'll be free
I will fly away with the cool breeze
And you will say to yourself:

"I made it"

Yours Truly, Ten Years from Now

Dear you,

From 10 years later

You have achieved some things in life

But I won't ruin it for you

You need to experience the surprise

The glory the fall and the rebirth

You will realize and embrace your humanity

Your taste buds will be grateful for the eclairs

And other fresh pastries from France

Your stomach will be grateful for the delicious dishes from Chicago

and cuisines from Portugal and Italy

Lastly, your ears and sight will be thankful

For those music festivals

That you always wanted to go to in Peru and Chile

Now, you might not like what I am about to tell you

And it will scare you

But

...You will stop jerking off to Hentai

I know it's hard and you will go through a

Horrible cold turkey

And yes it will feel like the end of the world

But you will make through buddy

Stay strong King!

All joking aside

You'll be relieved and you will be free
Your laptop will be virus free

You will have that one-on-one talk with you father
Won't tell you the result of it
It will be up to you to interpret it
You will throw a birthday party for yourself
So you can celebrate being alive
Your home is in South Central
Unless you do something about it...

Lastly you will tell your family that you love them
And you will mean it
And they'll know
You sister Mireya will cry
As she always does
Your teenage niece Sofia will be confused
But once you let her read your book
She'll understand your vulnerability

All of this happened or could happen
Or did not happen at all
I just imagined it for you
It's up to you to make it into your own reality
It's really up to you guy
It's up to you
It's all on you

If there is any advice I can give you,
It is to enjoy and fully embrace every moment

Reboot

I am leaving my cocoon
I'm shedding off my old skin
All the weight that I carried for the past 30 years
Is dropping
I'm no longer chained to my bed
I'm leaving my room everyday
I'm learning to walk on my own

And yes
I know I'll step on cracks
But that won't stop me
From getting where I want to be
I won't ask for permission anymore
I have a right to be here
No more floating around
Just being grounded
I'm feeling every step I take

And yes
I still have the memory of my undoing
But I no longer have the paranoia
The fear
Of repeating that cycle
I stop listening to their voices
I started listening to myself

My own voice

I have a right to be in my body
The barriers that the little boy in me built
Have started to crack
As I walk towards it with a hammer
To break it all down
I look forward to the day I can feel
The union of two bodies
Two souls
Two hearts
Beating as one

I am finally ascending

This new beginning is 30 years long overdue
But no matter
Because I finally started
And I really like where I am going

Outro

After everything that was written
And shared on the mic
I am now bear

I vomit everything that I could
Some will say I should have held it in
But I couldn't anymore

My vomit exposes the sickness that was inside me
But I decided to use it as an ink
On these pages

Makes me wonder about those who knew me
Before
How will they see me now?

There's nothing much left that I can give

The pen will go back hiding between the cushions

I'll be me on my own
But this time
Without the weight on my shoulders

Little boy's voice was heard

That's great for him
I'm listening to him clearly
Mime helped him find his voice
How ironic and funny
But they needed each other
Just like I needed paper, pen and pencil
Anything to record my being
And I'm going to miss them being in the same room
With me
Giving me the energy to speak up on these pages
To prove that I existed

Leaves me wondering if the reincarnation of me
Gets a hold of this book
Will it experience a deja vu?
Will it start remembering my journey?
The people that helped me?

I shouldn't stress about it
I need to rest
I deserve it
I've earn it

And I owe it to myself

What a cathartic journey this was

I now close this big chapter of my life

Thank you for reading me

Acknowledgments

Alex Alpharaoh - for igniting the poetry in me and starting this journey

Khuamel - for seeing the words in me and introducing me to Community Literacy Initiative

Hiram Sims - for believing in all us can write a book and getting out there in the world

Alex Petunia - for being a remarkable teacher and helping me shaped these poems

Ruddy Lopez, Lynda V. E. Crawford, Sakile Odomo, Chris Siders, Nicole Harmony, Brandon Elliot, Dianne Williams, Rita D. – for being my supportive peers during CLI Season 10 class

Cristian Perfas, Marc Cid & Hannah Pachman - for hosting open mic events at the Hey Hey Cafe

Brenda Vaca - for being a supportive friend and publisher while holding it down on the Post-Up open mic at Casa Verde

Lynda y Ruben - for being supportive and allowing their space Casa Verde at Whittier be a safe space for artists

No Pulp Poetry Club - for allowing their space to be a test ground for my poetry

Karo Ska - for supporting me on the process and being awesome teacher at Poetry 44 Class

Gia Civerolo - for motivating me to join the publishing class

Jessie Tovar - for being the first to allow me to be a feature and supporting poets all over LA by giving them spaces for their words to be heard

Amon Benavides - for helping me unravel my inner being during therapy sessions

Anne Marie Wells - for editing my poems

Elizabeth Weinschreider - for working with me on the covers of the book

Waseem Aziz - for working with me laying out the interior design of the book

Placebo - your music helped me kept myself from falling into the abyss

My family - for giving me the mental material to write and still manage to see the sun after all the storms

Me - for allowing myself to be an open book

You the reader - for picking up this book and reading this rollercoaster journey. Now is your turn to write.

About the Author

Juan Amador is a writer and performer from South Central Los Angeles. He graduated with a B.A. in Theater Arts at Loyola Marymount University.

His poems have been included in the literary journal Mobile Data Mag and anthologies from Beyond The Veil Press, Golden Foothill Press and Poetic Underground LLC Press.

Pimping My Trauma is his first book of poetry.
@thee_amador

About the Publisher

Riot of Roses Publishing House was founded in 2021 specifically to amplify the stories of historically silenced voices and narratives.

Xicana owned. Mujerista focused. For the people.

We publish books that heal and liberate.

Read our rebellion.

Find & follow us @riotofrosespublishing

Visit us at www.riotofrosespublishinghouse.com

RIOT OF ROSES
PUBLISHING HOUSE
SEJATNGA
UNCEDED TONGVA TERRITORY
SOUTH WHITTIER, CALIFORNIA

Milton Keynes UK
Ingram Content Group UK Ltd.
UKHW031913201124
451474UK00006B/529

9 781961 717220